10/68

ANF

B

35

③

22|10|6

Date of Return

DECISIONS FOR A DECADE

SENATOR
EDWARD M.
KENNEDY

DECISIONS FOR A DECADE

POLICIES AND PROGRAMS
FOR THE 1970s

Preface by George F. Kennan

LONDON
MICHAEL JOSEPH

Lines from *The Prophet*, by Kahlil Gibran, with the
permission of the publisher, Alfred A. Knopf, Inc.,
copyright 1923 by Kahlil Gibran; renewal copyright
1951 by Administrators C. T. A. of the Kahlil Gibran
Estate and Mary G. Gibran.

First published in Great Britain by
MICHAEL JOSEPH LTD
26 Bloomsbury Street
London WC1

Printed by offset lithography in Great Britain
by Hollen Street Press Ltd, Slough and bound by
James Burn at Esher, Surrey

To Joan; and to our children, Kara, Teddy and Patrick. The work is ours, the future theirs.

ACKNOWLEDGMENTS

My viewpoint on the problems discussed in this book has developed during my five and one-half years as United States Senator from Massachusetts. The life of the Senate offers continuous opportunities for the informal exchange of ideas. Senators talk to one another about public issues in the cloakroom during lulls in the proceedings, and on the way over to the Floor, as well as in the more formal debates and committee sessions. I have learned much from my colleagues, many of them thirty years my senior, who nevertheless have been most generous in sharing with me their wisdom and experience.

I am also fortunate to represent a state with a large number of colleges and universities, whose faculty members are passionately interested in public problems, given to new and imaginative approaches, and not at all shy

7

about trying to convert their latest thinking into public policy. I have made a regular practice of meeting with professors at the Massachusetts Institute of Technology, Harvard, Boston University, Amherst, Williams, Boston College, and Brandeis. I have benefited greatly from their viewpoints. This kind of interchange between the world of ideas and the world of government is a vital part of our national life.

Some of the chapters of this book have evolved from particular legislative projects in which I have been involved. For assistance in developing my position on Selective Service reform, I am especially grateful to Samuel P. Huntington of Harvard, Alan R. Novak, and Bradley Patterson, Jr., staff director of the President's Advisory Commission on Selective Service. I could not have begun to understand the needs and aspirations of American Negroes without the friendship of Aaron Henry and Charles Evers of Mississippi. I am grateful to professors Henry Kissinger and Thomas C. Schelling of Harvard for reviewing the material on European policy, and offering constructive suggestions. Barbara Ward, a brilliant and charming lady, was most helpful with the section on foreign aid, as were John Plank of the Brookings Institution, and former Ambassador to Chile Ralph Dungan with the section on Latin America.

Any attempt to work out future policies toward China and Asia presents a special challenge, since this is at once the chief focus of our current concern, and the part of the world about which we know the least. I received much help from former Ambassador to Japan, Edwin O. Reischauer, James Thomson, and Louis Sohn of Harvard, Doak

Barnett of Columbia and Lucien Pye of the Massachusetts Institute of Technology.

Finally, I want to thank Milton Gwirtzman, a Washington attorney who has worked closely with me ever since I first campaigned for the Senate, for his skill and judgment in research, and in drawing together the various chapters; and Jeff Greenfield, assistant to Senator Robert Kennedy, who lent his considerable talents to the final weeks of preparation of the manuscript.

Robert Manning and Richard N. Goodwin, men who have helped all the members of the Kennedy family, reviewed the manuscript and made numerous editorial suggestions. My Administrative Assistant in the Senate, David Burke, and my Legislative Assistants, James Flug and K. Dun Gifford have put tireless effort into work on many of these subjects. I am very grateful to all of them, as well as to my secretary, Angelique Voutselas, whose cheerfulness and dedication have helped mend both my back and my spirits over the last four years.

Needless to say, the responsibilities for any errors, of fact or judgment, are mine alone, along with my thanks to all who consider what I have to say.

Edward M. Kennedy
Boston, Massachusetts
January 19, 1968

PREFACE

The seriousness of the situation in which this country now
finds itself, both internally and externally, needs no emphasis at this point; nor does anyone need to make apolo-
gies or give explanations if, in approaching a volume of
this nature, he proceeds on the assumption that the United
States is a country in deep trouble. A whole series of facets
of our domestic life and our position in the world make
this evident. On the domestic front, there are such things
as the appalling alienation and demoralization of great
portions of the Negro population and the student youth;
the inability of the political system to control inflation; the
steady deterioration of our great cities; the chaos in trans-
portation; the rapid and continuing growth in crime; the
progressive pollution or destruction of natural environment. On the foreign scene, just to mention a few of the

11

problems, there is—even beyond the Vietnam involvement
—the general growth of anti-Americanism; our deteriorat-
ing foreign exchange situation; the crisis of NATO; the
highly dangerous and smoldering conflict in the Near East,
not to mention the problems of Greece and Cyprus; the
grotesque and hysterical xenophobia of Communist China;
and above all, the menace implied in the continuing proliferation of the power of disposal over nuclear weapons. In
their totality, these tendencies appear to be converging at
some early period—probably the 1970s—on a situation of
great national distress and danger. And their seriousness
lies not primarily in their own intractability as problems
(there are few of them to which answers or at least means
of alleviation are not theoretically conceivable, insofar as
things lie within the power of this country to influence
them) but rather in the fact that most of them have already
been before us for some time and yet have shown themselves resistant to successful treatment by the traditional
assumptions, methods, approaches and institutions of
American democracy. Evidently, the great crisis of American civilization that was foreseen by both Tocqueville and
Bryce when they looked at this country decades ago is now
upon us. Without a major recasting of traditional outlooks,
without much innovation and bold experimentation, without a thoroughgoing re-examination of both assumptions
and institutions, we are not likely to avoid within the coming decade a drastic deterioration both of our domestic
life and of our prosperity and security as a world power.

If responses of this sort are to be brought about peacefully and without damage to the basic structure of our democracy, they will have to be preceded by, and be the

products of, a national debate far more extensive, more searching and more responsible than anything we have seen in recent years. The question is: where is the initiative for this debate to come from? The intellectual journals are not enough. The mass media, serving by and large the needs of the advertisers rather than those of serious communication, are capable of lending themselves to the discussion of public problems only to a limited and inadequate degree—in that fragmentary, staccato and disorderly fashion that responds to advertising requirements. The gravity of the issues is such that leadership in this discussion should come, ideally, from the national political leadership; but it is evident that neither of two great political parties, concerned as they are to find the least common denominator of slogan and cliché around which to base their appeal, can be looked to for any useful initiative here; nor is the nation's highest personal office a place to which, if the experience of recent decades be taken as the criterion, one could hopefully look for this sort of stimulus and leadership. Yet it is highly desirable, and almost essential, that voices of people in senior and responsible public office take a prominent and even leading part in this sort of discussion. It is not enough just for intellectuals to debate among themselves. If such a debate is to be fruitful, it must bring to expression both the political experience that comes from the personal conquest of high political office and the authority that goes with its possession. Only in this way can the attempt to ascertain what is theoretically desirable be widened into the more useful, and eventually essential, effort to determine what is both theoretically desirable and politically conceivable. And only in this way, given the sort of press treatment to which the views of senior elected officials are exposed, can such a discussion be brought home to the consciousness of the man in the street and his responsible reaction to it enlisted in the form of his electoral behavior.

Necessary as this sort of contribution is if the nation is going to move with any hope of success into the vale of coming trial and danger, it is easier for the individual legislator, no doubt, to avoid it. Security in electoral office has only too often been won and long retained precisely by a studious refusal to take any meaningful part in the discussion of public problems—by a timid hiding behind the slogan and the commonplace, coupled with an adroit manipulation of the machinery of politics. It is to Senator Edward Kennedy's credit that he has eschewed this easy course and has not hesitated to explore, in this volume, a number of the most crucial and difficult problems of our national policy. The problems of student dissent and the draft, of race relations and Negro advancement, of foreign aid and of relations with both Latin America and Europe —all problems which, though affected in each case by the Vietnam involvement, will be present in one form or another even when and if that involvement is liquidated—are explored here in a spirit that is not only responsible but eminently practical. Particularly constructive and challenging is the initial chapter that deals with the possibilities for improving the American political system with a view to making it more responsive to the people who now have little sense of participation in it or expression through it.

The reader will find in this volume a great many suggestions for the improvement of our performance, domestically and in foreign affairs, but none that wanders into the realm of the fantastic or the unrealistically ideal, none which could not be seriously and realistically pursued within the existing institutional framework and in the face of attitudes and outlooks shared by at least large sections of our public opinion. In this, in their eminent practicality and sobriety, together with the liberal and tolerant approach that inspires them, lies their value. They do not cover, and obviously could not cover, the entire range of major problems now facing this country; and the critic may have his doubts, in some instances, as to whether one or the other of them goes far enough—whether, that is, wholly new concepts of what is thinkable and permissible in American practice will not have to come into being before certain of these problems can be mastered. But to sketch out wholly new concepts of this nature was not Senator Kennedy's purpose. His task was to suggest what could be done, and might suitably be done, within that framework of concept and customs and national mood which he, like every other elected official, has to accept and respect. Even within this framework there is much that can be done. This book gives a number of valuable suggestions as to what some of it might be; and these suggestions deserve serious attention. The service to the public interest that the book represents will be repaid if it evokes in response not just that cursory and passive acknowledgment which the views of public figures sometimes receive but a willingness on the part of other leaders of public opinion to take up the debate and to pursue these ideas to the point either of their clear rejection or their real acceptance, not just in public opinion but also in legislative and executive action.

George F. Kennan

15

CONTENTS

ACKNOWLEDGMENTS 7

PREFACE 11

INTRODUCTION 19

I. AT HOME 27

NEW DIRECTIONS IN AMERICAN
POLITICS 29

THE NEED TO SERVE 50

DISSENTING YOUTH: THE
DANGER AND THE PROMISE 66

THE FIRST DUTY OF GOVERNMENT
—THE CONTROL OF CRIME 81

THE RACIAL CRISIS 100

II. ABROAD   129

EUROPE: THE PARADOX OF
    SUCCESS   131

ASIA: THE PERILS OF
    OVERCOMMITMENT   148

LATIN AMERICA—AN APPROACH   173

OF WAR AND WANT   197

APPENDIX   216

18

INTRODUCTION

The decade of the 1970s begins the third century of the American Republic. The men who signed the Declaration of Independence in 1776 were fired by the conviction that free men could build a great nation, governed by their own wisdom. The coming decade will bring grave challenges to this conviction.

In two hundred years, this country has demonstrated its ability to overcome the obstacles we faced at our beginning—but these successes have not brought us ease. In the 1770s, we were a small nation, seeking our independence, surrounded by hostile powers. As we approach the 1970s, we are the most powerful country on earth; we can vastly improve the lives of any other people. We can also destroy them.

In the 1770s, we were primarily an agrarian country,

19

our greatest internal challenge was a wild and primitive frontier. In the 1970s, it is the consequences of our conquests—urbanization, automation and affluence—which will challenge us most.

We know today that our political structure, premised on the supremacy of individual rights, can endure and grow. But we also see that many of our best citizens, and an alarming number of our brightest, ablest youth, have lost faith in this system. They are urging others to step outside our political structure to redress their grievances; and their advice, if followed by enough of their fellows, threatens the vitality of our democratic process.

We know today that our system can produce a society in which most Americans enjoy a standard of living undreamed of throughout history. But for millions of our citizens, this affluence is a mockery of their own lives— lives of squalor, despair, and hopelessness. And this very affluence breeds among these poor a frustration and bitterness which has already triggered violence, and which threatens to do so again and again.

We know today that we can build a technology which can radically alter and ease our lives, bringing us leisure, comfort, and excitement. But we also know that this technology has corrupted our natural environment. And we are beginning to understand that the same machines which increase efficiency can also mean the invasion of privacy, the loss of jobs, and the erosion of individuality.

We know today that we can build a mighty nation, able to conquer any military threat, by any power. But we also know that this might has brought us neither peace nor security; that we must find alternatives to the constant amassing of armed might if we are to live in peace. And we know, too, as we fight a bloody and tragic war on the other side of the world, that armed might alone cannot buy security, or save us from spending lives and treasure in the madness of war; that we need to face—realistically and urgently—the job of resolving political disputes without resort to death and destruction.

These are the tasks we must face. But to state them does not guarantee that we shall accomplish them. When I was in college fifteen years ago, men were cataloging the challenges we faced in the postwar world; we too were told that they would soon be our responsibility. But we were given rhetoric—not the sense of the specific work to be done, and what roles we could play. So we settled—like most generations before us—into our homes and jobs, losing the spark of indignation and the commitment to change. We were content to settle for gradual progress where swift and bold change was required. We could not and did not see the need to grapple with these problems, until they had swelled into crisis. In the words of a French leader after France fell to the Nazis:

"We wanted to *have* more than we wanted to *give*. We spared effort, and met disaster."

Thus, America did not become serious about federal assistance to our burdened schools until the Soviet Union orbited Sputnik; only then did we begin to ask why our students were not learning. We did not see a crisis in medical care until more than half our elder citizens were found to be receiving inadequate attention and until hospital costs had soared. Then we passed Medicare. We saw no crisis of pollution until our rivers and air began to choke

21

with it. We were content to ignore the tragedy of our race problem until police dogs attacked Negro citizens of Birmingham; and we forgot our urban ghettos until they reminded us—with flames and guns—of the bitter people they sheltered. In short, the government we created was prevented, through our own neglect, from accomplishing the purposes set out in the preamble of the Constitution: domestic tranquillity, the general welfare, justice, and a more perfect Union. Failure will not mean simply that a few Americans will be denied their rights, or that a small part of our security will be lost. Failure now may well rip apart the threads of American greatness. We cannot, with all our wealth, reform our political and economic life if our best young minds and our poorest citizens conclude—as some are now doing—that the American system is no longer worth saving. The next decade will—literally—determine the vitality of the root beliefs of American democracy.

If we are to avoid defeat, we must know clearly what we must do, and how we are to do it. This requires a willingness to think differently, and to challenge accepted notions which have proven either false or outmoded. It also requires patience.

Thus, the criticisms I make in these pages are not of this Administration, nor of its predecessors, but of national attitudes which have forced inadequate policies. If we are to change these policies, we must first challenge and change these attitudes. This book is not a document addressed to the 1968 campaign, but to the next Administration of this country, and the one that follows it. For the man elected President this year will begin to confront the 1970s—the dangers, and the promise, that the 200th year of American life will bring. He will have to call upon the coming generation to face these challenges—and this will require understanding. He will have to grapple with technological and economic change before this change outstrips our ability to affect it—and this will require action. He will have to shape our responses to a new and difficult world—and this will require prudence.

When we are told that "the present situation of the world is indeed without a parallel, and that of our own country full of difficulties," we know this is true. But this warning was offered not by a contemporary, but by James Madison in his inaugural address more than 150 years ago. So the question is not whether we are challenged, but how, and what we are to do about it.

To some, the condition of modern America is a cause for despair or pessimism. To some, the coming decade appears one of insurmountable problems. I do not believe this is the case. This nation has always met and conquered the threats it has faced—to its survival, to its unity, to its economic security. The difficulties the 1970s will bring are ones which we, acting together, can help resolve. As Franklin D. Roosevelt said: "These dark days will be worth all they cost us if they teach us that our true destiny is not to be ministered unto, but to minister to ourselves and our fellow men." This is the lesson we must have before us as we approach the third American century.

DECISIONS FOR A DECADE

PART I

AT HOME

NEW DIRECTIONS IN
AMERICAN POLITICS

The tasks of the 1970s will require sweeping changes in
the attitudes of Americans: toward poverty, toward other
races and nations, toward the character of their own lives.
But these changes cannot be *imposed* on our citizens—that
is not the business of free government. Support for new
policies must develop out of a genuine dialogue between
those in public life and those they represent. Thus, as a
precondition to any effective action, we will need political
leadership responsive to its citizens, respected by those it
serves, able to translate the wishes of the people into action. This, after all, is the reason for democracy. Free
speech, press, and assembly—the First Amendment rights
of expression—are not just ends in themselves. They exist

29

so that people can peacefully bring about the political and social changes they desire.

We cannot, then, move ahead with policies for the 1970s unless we are sure that our political system is indeed responsive to the people of our country—and unless the people themselves feel that the system is listening to them. This is not the case today. Far too many Americans, of all classes and ages, have come to believe that the political process has no place in it for them. Why is this so; and what can be done?

At first glance, our political system appears fully responsive to its people. Expression and activity are more wide open than at any other time in our history. At the start of the Republic, critics of government were often severely punished by the now-discredited Sedition Act, and by stringent state libel laws. The vote was restricted to white, male property owners; Senators and even Presidents were elected without a chance for popular vote.

Today, critics of government are vigorously protected under the First Amendment—not only from punishment, but even from libel suits by public officials angered at intemperate attacks. The fear of joining "controversial" organizations, so predominant during the 1950s, has substantially vanished. More important, the right to vote has been greatly expanded, by both judicial interpretations of the Constitution and by legislative action. Women and Negroes both have the vote, and with the passage of the 1965 Voting Rights Act, the legal obstacles to Negro voting in the South have largely been removed. Between 1965 and 1967, more than 500,000 Negroes in five Deep South states

30

registered to vote for the first time. And soon thereafter, the poll tax was abolished.[1]

Perhaps most important, the votes of all citizens will soon be equal. Until a few years ago, citizens of large cities and suburbs were in effect second-class citizens—because their representatives had as little as one-twentieth the voting power as those from small towns and rural areas. This pattern, commonplace both in our House of Representatives and in almost all state legislatures, meant that the citizens of this country were unequal in the forum where public policy was made. With the Supreme Court's "one-man-one-vote" decisions, with the Senate's refusal to accept delay in implementing this rule, and with the work of citizens throughout the United States, Americans are beginning to win their fair voice in our legislatures.

Thus, we see our people with more freedom to speak, to criticize, to vote, and to influence, than at any other time. And when we add to this the public opinion polls, the commentary and "listen-talk" shows on radio and television, and the growth of private associations devoted to specific aims and goals (at last count more than 20,000 of them), it may well seem that as a people we are more involved in public affairs than we ever have been.

But this optimism is too simple: it reflects a cherished American belief that if everyone has the right to vote for his representatives, to petition his government, and if the

[1] Congress outlawed the poll tax in federal elections only in 1965. I proposed an amendment outlawing that tax altogether, and while it failed in the Senate by four votes, Congress did direct that the tax be challenged in Court by the Attorney General. Shortly thereafter, the Supreme Court in Harper v. Board of Elections 383 U.S. 663 (1966) abolished that barrier to public participation.

31

press and the interest groups keep careful watch on the affairs of state, the public's voice will be heard and the government will respond. This is a worthy theory, and has important elements of truth—but it is a false description of the political picture today.

THE NARROWING OF DEMOCRACY

The fact of the matter is that for many Americans, government does not *seem* close to them. It is not a process in which they feel welcome. It is, instead, a distant, often hostile system, making decisions for them, not with them. And for too many Americans, the response to this feeling is either to shun the public life, or else to disrupt it.

The roots of this disturbing belief are many. The first is the sheer growth of government, from a group of legislators infrequently assembling for discussion and voting, into a massive machine which affects every aspect of our national life. The classic system of representative democracy has bogged down badly in the sheer size of our time. Edmund Burke, whose 1774 letter to his Bristol constituents eloquently expresses the duty of a legislator, had 5000 constituents. I have 5,500,000. Burke's electors were men with a common background and common interests. Mine embrace widely divergent interests, beliefs, and goals. Even Congressmen often must take into account the views of almost 500,000 people. With such a vast number of constituents, how can a public official, however conscientious, realistically get to know those who elect him to office? And, more important, how can a private citizen feel that a Congressman is at all interested in his personal problems or views? The blunt answer is, he can't. If I spent one minute with each of my constituents, I would do nothing else, all day, every day, for more than ten years.

But growth is only one part of the problem. For with growth has come complexity; a staggering bureaucracy (on all levels of government) which, although made up of dedicated and hardworking people, often seems to a private citizen—and even to a public official—as an indifferent, uncontrollable machine. With more than 11,500,000 employees working for all levels of government, the average citizen must depend for help on the decisions of people he neither elects, nor knows, nor even sees. When Abraham Lincoln was President, it was possible for an ordinary citizen to walk into his office with a grievance or a request, and get a hearing. Today, that citizen is lucky to see a human being; his claim is usually processed by a computer. This is not the fault of the individual civil servant. He does the best he can; but the population he must serve is so large requests come in a steady stream. He cannot treat each one with the urgency it has for the citizen who presents it.

Citizens with a grievance, however justified—often find they get unsatisfactory response from this bureaucracy. Indifference to their complaints—often involving severe hardships—is not uncommon. A letter wrongly addressed and departments which refer inquiries to others out of habit often drive people to despair. Every Congressman and Senator, consequently, finds much of his staff's time and effort consumed by "casework"—the business of interceding on behalf of constituents before government agencies. But even our expression of interest is no guarantee.

I often have the feeling that my inquiry is answered by the same person who made the decision in the first place. I imagine if I went over to the agency's office and pounded on the table I might get results. But with more than three hundred requests for casework each week, I would have little time to perform my legislative function.

It is no wonder that citizens who have been bruised in their dealings with government tend to see it functioning not as a public servant, but as a master, without concern for the people. If this feeling can be sparked by relatively simple matters, such as a pension check or a request for local action, how much more distant must government seem when it makes decisions about the "big issues"—of war, defense, and foreign affairs?

Not long ago, government, even at the federal level, was dealing mostly with issues about which people knew, and about which they felt deeply. Protection of workers, government-supported unemployment insurance; these are issues about which ordinary citizens had an opinion. They might not understand the details, but at least they understood the broad issues. But how do citizens make a decision on government support for a supersonic transport? How do the people back home inform themselves about the wisdom of an antiballistic missile system? What sense does it make to ask for views on technical assistance grants to developing nations for economic planning? With the expansion of government responsibility, and the growing complexity of the modern world, Congressmen themselves —not to mention their constituents—are confronted with a bewildering array of reports, statistics, hearings, and proposals which no legislator, no matter how energetic, can fully follow.

One example can illustrate this sense of helplessness. A New Jersey Congressman not long ago sent out a questionnaire, asking his constituents' views on budget cuts, Vietnam policy, and other issues. He received a reply which read: "I can't answer these questions—why do you think I sent you to Washington?"

This complexity is fused with a political process which itself seems divorced from the people. When parties seem to choose candidates at a distance from the electorate, and when we glimpse our prospective leaders only in 30-second television commercials designed to impress rather than to inform, we have a truly disturbing picture. We see a government far out of human proportions, deciding issues of indecipherable complexity, by people who the electors do not know, and rarely hear.

THE CONSEQUENCES OF ALIENATION

This concern for the condition of American politics is far from academic. It is beginning to have two serious consequences which do not promise well for the future health of our nation.

The first is indifference; that "you-can't-fight-city-hall" sense which separates citizens from politics, and inspires an even stronger sense that politics is meaningless, citizens powerless and participation in public affairs useless. This nation—with the highest literacy rate in the world, and with unparalleled communications—has the lowest voting rate of any industrialized nation. Only 60 percent of our eligible voters cast their ballots in the 1964 presidential election, compared with national turnouts of well over 80 percent in Britain, 84 percent in Sweden, 74 percent in Japan and 70 percent in Chile. In non-presidential years, the figure drops even further. Less than 53,000,000 of more than 114,000,000 eligible voters cast ballots for Congressmen in the 1966 election.

This indifference can often lead to unexpected and sudden rebellions against important decisions which, in the eyes of the electorate, were taken by remote and distant governments. Many states, struggling to tap public resources for vital programs, have found the voters rejecting important tax and spending programs. At least 25 percent of school bond issues have been rejected over the last ten years, and in the elections in the middle of 1967, the rate rose to 35 percent.

But this indifference and hostility is overshadowed by a second consequence of political isolation: the growing belief that the peaceful resolution of disputes by the process of debate, discussion and voting, is no longer effective, and that only dramatic action *outside* the traditional political framework can win demands.

A new political process is rising, based on the inadequacies of the traditional structure. The barricades of Paris have gone up from the campus at Berkeley to the Common at Boston. The stronghold of this new political style is the college campus, illustrated by the fact that 15 percent of American college students participated last year in at least one demonstration. But we also see housewives picketing supermarkets and scuffling with police in front of the White House; farmers dumping milk; tenants and teachers striking; and police and firemen refusing to work in major cities.

Most of these direct protests are legal. All of them are considered by the participants as desirable, even necessary methods of dramatizing deep-seated grievances. (Nothing more clearly demonstrates this than to go back to the source of modern direct-action protests; the non-violent sit-ins over civil rights in the South.) But the spread of such tactics should warn us of the feeling behind them: the sense that the traditional American political process is no longer enough. It is one thing for Southern Negroes, exploited, oppressed, and voteless, to demonstrate in the face of an unconstitutional, unyielding system. It is another for articulate, even influential citizens to believe that they can win a fair hearing only if they present their issues in dramatic, unorthodox ways. And, as I shall discuss in Chapter III, it is difficult to prevent direct action from becoming civil disobedience, and civil disobedience from becoming violent disruption of the rights of others.

Our traditional institutions of representative democracy have served us well, in good times and bad. They contain too much that is sound and useful to be permitted to be swallowed up in the uncertainties of direct action. We want to encourage those with grievances to present their views peacefully, but we cannot urge a return to traditional structures unless we make sure they are effective. It makes no sense to urge an aggrieved citizen to write his Senator if the Senator cannot give a speedy and satisfactory answer.

37

It makes no sense to go through channels if they are clogged, or lead only to confusion and delay.

THE TASKS AHEAD

I believe that much can be done over the next few years to make government more responsive to people. The effort requires two major tasks: first, the modernization of traditional political structures, and second, the creation of new political institutions, to bring people and politics closer together and give more authentic power to our citizens.

We can start with the most important office of all, the Presidency. With the growth of the Executive Branch's authority, the President carries with him the goals of every citizen. His responsibilities, his power of life and death over the world, make him, more than anyone else, the man whose decisions most forcefully and directly affect our lives. If they are to feel an affinity to him that is more than the passive relationship of ruled to ruler, the people must have a far greater role than they do now in selecting the man who is to hold this office.

Our system of selecting presidential nominees by national conventions, begun in the period of Jacksonian Democracy, had this purpose. Instead of being selected by members of the elite, Presidents were to be chosen by delegates of the members of the parties. But the average person watching a convention on television today has about as much feeling of personal participation as watching a professional football game. Only rarely has he voted for those who are his delegates, and as a result, his selection of a President is limited to a choice between two men selected for him by strangers.

The most effective method of increasing participation is to increase the use of presidential primaries, thus giving citizens a wider range of choices within their own party prior to the November election. Two years ago, we in Massachusetts passed a new primary law binding delegates to vote for the winner of the presidential preference primary on the first ballot. (Thereafter, they are free to make their choices, thus preserving the advantages of a flexible convention.) We thus joined a handful of other states, such as Wisconsin, Oregon, Nebraska and California, where presidential primaries can be a real opportunity for democracy.[2]

It is apparent, from the tremendous interest these primaries arouse, that the American people would welcome the opportunity to participate more fully in the selection of their President. If presidential primaries were extended to other states, it would make this participation a reality. It would also permit people with strong views on national and world affairs to work through the traditional two-party system to gain adherents for their views. I am not suggesting a national primary, or the abandonment of the conventions' role in choosing the nominees, but rather the

[2] Fifteen states elect convention delegates by primaries, but in most of these, delegates are not instructed by the voters. A few states give voters a chance to express their preference as to a presidential nominee, but do not require the delegates to heed it. Thus, although President Kennedy won the West Virginia primary in 1960, he received only 15 out of 25 votes from the West Virginia delegation.

more effective instruction of delegates by party members.

To increase the number of primaries would cost money, and could, under present conditions, aggravate the trend by which only wealthy men or those with wealthy backers can run for President. I think we must be realistic about the fact that in a country this large, it takes a great deal of money to run for major office. That is why we must make it easier for candidates to raise money, by allowing tax deductions for political contributions up to, say, $100; and by allowing primary candidates access to free television and radio time, to cut down the single largest item of campaign expense. Structured in this way, the presidential primary could well become an effective and practical mechanism for bringing dissidents back into the mainstream of representative democracy.

Next we should look at the legislative elections. The one remaining barrier to the true realization of the "one-man-one-vote" principle is the gerrymandering of legislative districts, a process outlawed by Congress long ago but permitted in practice for the last forty years. Gerrymandering is the deliberate drawing of district lines to make them "safe" for one political party or another. In securing this purpose, however, it has diluted the quality of representation.

If a legislator is "safe" from competition, or if he represents groups with the same economic and political beliefs, he does not have to change his ideas or respond to the needs of the broader population. He can rest content with a mediocre, absentee performance, knowing he will be returned to office. And as he is returned, year after year, the seniority system gives him immense control over people from other parts of the country whose views he need not heed at all.

It can be argued that contiguous and homogenous areas should have their own representation—that Brooklyn's Bedford-Stuyvesant, for example, a community of 400,000 Negroes, deserves a Congressman as much as Maryland's Eastern Shore or Michigan's Upper Peninsula. But this does not justify the continued use of rotten boroughs or artificially created units of ethnic, religious, and economic groupings created for political purposes. Especially in Congress, we need men who are responsive to the needs of a wide variety of interests and do not think in single-minded, parochial terms.

Congress should move toward ending this distortion of political interests by requiring that districts be "as compact as possible."[3] The elections for Congress would give new importance to districts of broadly diverse groups.

In addition to electing officials, our people need to be heard more effectively in the resolution of issues. We should increase the use of referenda on national and world issues during election campaigns. It may be true, for example, that the war in Vietnam has little to do with a municipal election, but as the voting in Cambridge, Massachusetts, and San Francisco, California, in the fall of 1967 showed, people want to express themselves on this issue (San Francisco enjoyed the highest turnout in years for a local election). Indeed, fusing a vote on candidates with a vote on issues would provide a more accurate gauge

[3] This proposal was accepted by the Senate in the first session of the 90th Congress, but House-Senate differences resulted in its abandonment.

41

of what people were voting for, and could result in more issue-oriented campaigns.

We could also extend the use of public opinion polls. As Winston Churchill once said, "We live in the temperamental atmosphere of the Gallup Poll, always feeling our own pulse and taking our own temperature." Public officials and commentators are at times obsessed with the public temperament; the entire climate of national affairs, indeed the political effectiveness of the Presidency itself, has been influenced by the job rating the pollsters give a President. We do this, of course, because as a democracy, we want to know how people think, and a poll is considered the next best thing to a referendum or an election. Yet, a poll, scientific as its sampling is, relies on, at most, a few thousand people to speak the thoughts of many millions. With today's technology, we could develop a system where everyone with access to a television set would be able to watch a discussion or debate on a current issue and then, by dialing a number of their telephone or by punching a response on a box hooked to the set, could record their opinion. It would not be just a simple yes or no. It would take into account gradations of viewpoint, requests for more information, or their sense that a question or proposition has been poorly phrased.

The new polls and referenda I am suggesting would not be binding decisions. They would not be substituted for the representative's vote, or relieve him of the responsibility of applying his own judgment and consulting his own conscience. They would merely measure public opinion more broadly and effectively than the polls we follow so carefully now, and, more importantly, give everyone the chance to take part in the polling process.

There will, of course, remain many issues too complex for informal public opinion. But to those who fear the greater participation of the mass of electorate, I would point out that we will soon have the best-informed citizens in the history of the world. By the mid-1970s over half the voters in the United States will have gone to college. They will have much more leisure time with which to inform themselves. They will have access to information retrieval and learning systems of an extremely advanced type. Through inexpensive computers installed in their homes, they will be able to get information from the Library of Congress in a shorter time than even the Librarian of Congress can today. With the feeling that their views are being sought, they will inform themselves.

Another step we can take, on all levels of government, is to provide a check on the bureaucracies which, for many citizens, are now the only link to the process of decision-making. Several nations have already created an office of *ombudsman,* or "public protector," first seen in Sweden in 1809, and since spread to the other Scandinavian countries, New Zealand, West Germany, Japan, Yugoslavia, and to Nassau County, New York. In essence, the public protector is nothing more than a processor of complaints against the government. It is his job to examine cases where officials have ignored or mishandled a citizen's grievance. He has no official power, except that of reprimand. But, through publicity, through the influence of his office, and through his access to agency and legislative leaders, he has the power to help a citizen mistreated by the government.

A public protector—an agency funded by the government but responsible directly to the citizenry—would provide the citizen with an effective mechanism for breaking through

43

the often jammed machinery of government. By representing citizens in their claims against government, by investigating complaints, by discovering unfair administration of rules, and by revealing government misconduct to the people, a public protector would make bureaucracy more accountable.

NEW FORUMS FOR DEMOCRACY

These innovations to control bureaucracy, to extend voter participation, to provide new mechanisms of expression and an equally effective voice for all voters, will help. But they cannot, by themselves, check the sense of helplessness which many Americans feel toward their units of government. We also require new political *structures*, to put government back into the hands of the people; to provide, in short, real political power in small, connected groups in a neighborhood or community.

This is hardly a radical idea. It is at the root of New England "town meeting" democracy which we all honor in its theory. It is that sense of control which exists today in small towns and suburbs, where citizens know their officials, set educational policy, and debate the size of the budget. That sense of control has largely vanished in our large cities, where the size of government has swelled, and grown far too powerful for separate neighborhoods and citizens to affect.

What happens today is that decisions, whether about roads, or urban renewal, or playgrounds, are made "downtown," away from the communities where people will be affected by them. It is a product in part of the political corruption which was rampant in big cities fifty years ago and which caused reformers to cry, "Take politics out of city government." This trend, which placed planning decisions in "apolitical" bureaucracies, may have helped to end corruption, but look at what else it did: If an urban renewal project was planned for a ghetto (or for that matter, an established "ethnic" community) that decision would be made by the planners. Usually these were white, middle-class, highly educated men with little personal knowledge of the neighborhoods in their city. Too often, the "apolitical decision" to build a road or to tear down a street was made without the approval or participation of the neighborhood.

Clearly this decision *was* political, in the sense that it affected, drastically, the life of a community. When we see people staging disruptive rallies outside City Hall, or shouting at a hearing, we should remember this background; and understand the importance of putting power back where the people are.

One way to accomplish this is the use of organized community meetings, on a small-scale basis, to discuss neighborhood problems and plan for action. At present, a wide variety of groups, ranging from welfare recipients to church leaders, are working in communities to focus on problems. If they were to group together for regular community meetings, they would become a forum where the voice of a neighborhood would be heard. In this effort, they could have the support of a variety of professional men who have come to realize that the values of the people affected must be of prime concern. For example, lawyers now work in Office of Economic Opportunity Neighborhood Legal Centers; doctors are working in community medical services projects throughout cities; and city planners, as a recent American Institute of Planning study showed, are deeply concerned that decisions take into account the needs of all the citizens. These professionals could act as advocates at community meetings, channeling grievances into specific complaints and requests for city agencies to consider. (Some cities might wish to experiment with paid planners, elected in neighborhood meetings, responsible not to the city, but to the neighborhood itself.)

These community meetings could serve to express opinion; but we also require local units of government, subdivided into far smaller units than cities or counties. When we remember that New York, Los Angeles, and Chicago each has larger populations than America did in 1789, we can understand how much we have grown—and how distant government has become. What we need, in a favorite phrase of Thomas Jefferson, is to "divide the counties into wards," creating small units of government, with real power, within our established boundaries.

These organizations, community centers, or "citizen assemblies," would be open to all citizens of a neighborhood. They would have the power to chart the course of the neighborhood's public policy; decide the policies and personnel of Head Start programs, the placement of recreational facilities, the kinds of job-training programs, the problems with city housing in the neighborhood. Such an organization would be a bridge between the city and the people, because it would be the people themselves, expressing their commitment to their communities—a commitment

46

to build, not to burn or to riot as a last desperate act of assertion.

Last year, I introduced a series of amendments to the War on Poverty legislation to encourage such community organization by allowing the federal government to fund neighborhood centers for the poor. While the program passed by Congress was on a small scale, it should be allowed to grow, until no city in the nation is hampered in developing such institutions by lack of financial resources.

Nowhere would such neighborhood groups work more effectively than in the schools. Unlike their counterparts in village and suburbs, parents in big cities have little or no say in decisions about education. Yet they are passionately, profoundly concerned about their children's schools. Without involvement, the alternative is protest, the kind that brought 500,000 Negro children out of New York schools in 1964, and which has caused disruption in Boston, Chicago, and other large cities, in the form of boycotts, teacher strikes, and bitter disputes.

We are now beginning to understand that we must decentralize the process of education, to make it meaningful for children and parents. Experiments with neighborhood school boards are already beginning, where parent-elected boards will largely determine policy. More controversial proposals are in the offing. In Boston, Negro parents are running two of their own schools. City-wide decentralization of the school system for New York has been proposed by McGeorge Bundy, head of the Ford Foundation.

It seems to me that democratically elected groups, exercising the power to affect educational policy, would be another effective means for providing citizens with legitimate

47

political power. Like the neighborhood centers and community meetings, these school committees would not work smoothly or quietly. They would air the same kinds of grievances that have sparked bitterness, protest, violence, and death—but they would do it peacefully. There would be disputes; there would be abuse of power. They would not prevent corruption. But there would also be more authentic citizen power than we now have. For individuals would be directly involved in the making of public decisions, many for the first time in their lives, and this would increase their commitment to their governments.

Indeed, within these centers, *political* involvement would grow; particularly where political parties began once again to be directly concerned with community affairs. It is no secret that local political parties, with a shrinking number of exceptions, are losing their hold on our citizens. The patronage they control is drying up. The social services they used to offer have been replaced by government programs, or rendered unnecessary by the growing affluence of the community. Most citizens consider them simply institutions for the gaining and keeping of political power, something in which they are scarcely interested. When the time comes that citizens are able to form a direct relation with candidates through television, and even vote by foolproof electronic means from their own homes, local political organizations, as we know them, could atrophy.

There must be work for political parties to do between elections as well as in campaigns. They must become active in youth activities, poverty programs and health and hospital work. Their local headquarters could offer legal services and tax advice to the poor. They might use as a model

48

the work now being done by the Young Democrats of Massachusetts, the senior Democratic parties in New York and Michigan, and by Students for a Democratic Society in poverty areas. If political parties did this, they would find people beginning to look on them with more than a cynical wariness.

These proposals may sound radical, but they express, in fact, nothing more than Jefferson's goal of almost two hundred years ago: for "every man to be a sharer in the direction of his ward-republic, and to feel he is a participant in the governing of his affairs, not merely on Election Day, one day a year, but every day."

They encompass—both in the extension of traditional structures and the creation of new ones—the central notion that our system of democracy is not helplessly corrupt or obsolete. It has, in my view, enough flexibility to change, grow, and renew itself.

Today is not the first time we have faced the challenge of making our government more responsive. That is why we created political parties in the first place. That is why we extended the franchise, directly elected Senators, struck down poll taxes, and now demand that the vote of all count equally. Today the challenge is different. It is to overcome the growth of our system, and to give to our citizens the ability to participate directly in the shaping of public policy. We can, if we make the effort, bring back to the people the realization that they are, in Jefferson's words, the "depositories of the ultimate powers of the society." They—all of us—will need this realization to accomplish the work of the next decade.

49

THE NEED TO SERVE

The coming decade will, unhappily, still see the nations of the world spending much of their resources on the weapons of death. The tensions of the cold war, national rivalries, and the resort to armed violence will hopefully begin to disappear; but we will still have to maintain and equip large armies. And therefore it is necessary that we in the United States examine with care the basis on which we will select young men for military service.

Throughout modern history, nations have required their young to fight wars for them as an obligation of citizenship. Traditionally, military service has been accepted as a duty; particularly when a nation claims to be fighting for its survival, or for the peace of the world. In World War II, for example, men who were physically unfit for service were pariahs, and resistance to the draft was negligible. In the

Korean War, when I was in the military, men who had been drafted out of college served with little overt complaint. Today, however, the draft is the target of widespread and growing attack.

In its most extreme form, men are refusing to cooperate with the Selective Service System, in protest both against the Vietnam war, and against the whole system of the draft. More than eighty offices are operating throughout the country to counsel young men on how to avoid, delay, or resist induction. Booklets on *How to Beat the Draft* are doing brisk business. Student and underground newspapers run a column on draft evasion (written under the pseudonym "General Marsbars"). Draft cards are kindling, and anti-war rallies feature the chant "Hell No, We Won't Go." Hundreds of students on campuses sign declarations announcing their intention to refuse military service. With Selective Service attempting to punish dissenters by drafting them, and with the indictment of prominent citizens for assisting draft resistance, the draft has become the major civil liberties issue of the Vietnam war.

We read of these manifestations in the newspapers almost every day. But the less visible forms of opposition are far more widespread, and far more corrosive. For one thing, military service is regarded by a growing minority as the worst of all possible worlds; a fate to be avoided at almost any cost. Young men change their careers, their schools, and even their marriage plans to reduce their chances of service; among some young couples, children are called "war babies." The practice of making university education a draft exemption prompted Kingman Brewster, Jr., president of Yale University and a member of the President's

51

Advisory Commission on Selective Service, to attack "a cynical avoidance of service, a corruption of the aims of education, and a tarnishing of the national spirit."

It is undeniable that some who oppose the draft do so purely on grounds of personal convenience. They would object to service no matter what the cause, and no matter how fair the system. But we should also recognize that much of the opposition and much of the evasion is triggered by the way the draft works. The plain fact is, our selective service system is an obsolete, irrational and wholly unfair institution. Its recruitment system is locked into arbitrary, incomprehensible patterns of operation.

It is not enough to argue that millions of older Americans went through the draft in former years, and to complain is somehow unpatriotic. We owe it to those who serve, and to ourselves, to modernize the system, and to provide a far broader range of possibility for our young men.

Many who oppose the draft are willing and eager to serve their society. If our system could tap this sense of obligation, today's cynicism might be replaced by a surge of youthful energy that would demonstrate to the older generation the pride that youth does have in its country.

A VOLUNTEER ARMY?

We should recognize, at the outset, that the draft is inevitably a form of drastic compulsion over the lives of individuals. Whether or not it is also a "privilege," military service is, short of criminal punishment, the strongest degree of control that government has over citizens. To take a young man away from his home, his job, and his family for two or three years, however necessary it may be, is a stringent interference with his life.

Given this compulsion, it is understandable that great interest has been shown in the possibility of abolishing the draft in favor of an all-volunteer army. This proposal has won the support of youth groups from all political shades—from Students for a Democratic Society to the National Student Association to the Young Americans for Freedom, and of many members of Congress. They point out that more than 60 percent of our military manpower is met through enlistments. If we raised the pay of soldiers and provided post-military incentives, they argue, we could perhaps persuade others to join the service voluntarily, and eliminate the need for compulsory service.

I think this proposal deserves serious consideration. If we could meet manpower needs, at reasonable costs, voluntarily, it seems unjustifiable that we should continue the uncertainties and the hardships that the draft can cause. And much as I believe in the concept of public service, I am not persuaded that this obligation can only be exercised through the military. Further, the social benefits of the Army, and the opportunities it offers, are not a case for compelling service. Many young Americans will continue to join the Armed Forces because they offer opportunity they cannot find elsewhere. The service has largely eliminated racism, and it offers education to veterans. But with anti-poverty programs, scholarship aids and other outside benefits, it hardly seems that *compulsory* military service should be forced on those who can gain social benefits elsewhere. So I would hope that we carefully consider the

53

possibility of meeting our manpower needs without compulsion at a reasonable cost—thus eliminating the pressures compelled military service can breed.

But until we know more clearly how much it would cost and what the likely consequences are, ending the draft is not a realistic policy for the next decade. First, cost estimates are highly uncertain; they range from $4,000,000,000 to $20,000,000,000 a year. That upper figure is a high price to pay, set alongside other national matters such as abolishing slums, providing better job and educational opportunities, and ending the pollution of our air and water. Further, my own conversations with college students lead me to question the character of any volunteer army. Those students who advocate a volunteer Army instead of a draft almost invariably admit *they* would not volunteer. This suggests strongly that in an all-volunteer Army, the present economic inequality in the draft would be magnified—that our soldiers would come from the lower economic classes —and that we would have a kind of platonic guard of permanent military men, paid to fight the wars of our society.

Throughout this century, our country has made its military commitments with the knowledge that a large burden of the fighting would be borne by men conscripted from all classes of civilian life. Our leaders have always known that they were accountable to the people for the acts that sent their sons to war. This knowledge has not always proven a check upon excessive military involvement, but it has prevented us from galloping off to battle precipitously. We did not enter World War I until our ships were sunk, nor World War II until we were attacked directly. Since that time, we

54

have dispatched military supplies, advisors, and other aid with great frequency. But the American boy, representing our ultimate commitment, has been used in combat only sparingly.

FLAWS IN THE DRAFT

These are the objections which a volunteer army proposal must answer. The more immediate challenge, however, is to reform our present Selective Service System.

The chief problems can be stated briefly:

First, it *is* selective, not universal. By 1970 there will be more than 15,000,000 men between the ages of eighteen and twenty-four. Our armed forces could not accommodate all these young men even if they wanted to. The task, then, is to find a way of selecting the needed draftees from this enormous pool without racial or economic discrimination.

Second, the drafting of oldest men first creates a maximum of uncertainty in the lives of young men. Since induction occurs when most young men are married or just starting their careers, the disruption it causes is severe. According to a recent survey on student stress, almost all male students regard the draft as a prime source of pressure, because, as one put it, "We don't know what's going to happen to us." And those classified 1-A find job prospects slim. Some 25 percent of those classed as draft-eligible are turned down for jobs because of their draft status. In fact, I spoke to one young man who could have gotten a deferment if he had a job; he was the sole support of his mother.

55

But he could not get a job because he was 1-A. If induction took place before careers were begun, the disruption would be minimized.

Third, the lack of real national standards means that the 4000 local draft boards around the country can make their own policy, with suggestions and recommendations from national headquarters. The result is a total sense of arbitrariness. Peace Corps volunteers may be deferred in New York, but drafted in Nebraska. Two men with the same physical ailment get totally different treatment by different boards. Even the criteria for "national interest" deferments are interpreted differently by different boards. The result is a sense of absolute confusion. Young men file for status on the basis of misinformation; they move in a world out of Kafka, where no one seems to know what rules are binding, what suggestions are only advisory, and what standards local boards may use.

Finally, the crazy-quilt system of deferments—for education, family status, and occupation—has spawned a staggering amount of confusion and irrationality, as well as the "cynical avoidance of service" which disturbed Yale's President Brewster. We give mandatory deferments to students in good standing in four-year colleges and universities; but not to those in junior colleges and two-year colleges. We virtually ignore the more than one million young men, mostly of lower economic background, who are in vocational training, and who are as hard-working and deserving as their more affluent counterparts. But their status is deemed inferior. They must be in training for so-called essential or critical skills and, even then, their local boards

56

can draft them if the quota is unfilled.[1] From my talks with these young men, I know they *feel* mistreated—as though this government really did not mean what it says about equality of opportunity.

Further, many in college pyramid their deferment into a graduate deferment; or they marry and have a family to reduce their chances of military service; or they take a job which is "in the national interest," not out of dedication, but out of avoidance.[2]

---

[1] This recent change in the Selective Service regulations is clearly against the intent of the Senate, which stated in its report accompanying the 1967 draft extension bill:

"If student deferments are to be continued, the Committee believes that apprentices should be permitted to qualify for deferment under conditions no more restrictive than those applicable to undergraduate college deferments."

They also appear to ignore the words of the Senate floor manager of the Conference Report, Senator Richard B. Russell, the Chairman of the Armed Services Committee:

"It is my understanding of the position of the Senate conferees that apprentices are entitled to exactly the same treatment (as college students)."

[2] Under the draft revisions passed in 1967, graduate deferments are abolished, *but* the National Security Council is given the obligation to recommend graduate student deferments in certain fields of study. The Council is also directed to recommend occupational deferments if it determines them to be in the national interest. At this writing, the National Security Council has been asked by Selective Service to grant deferments to graduate students in the fields of mathematics, engineering, natural science, and health. Of the nearly 150,000 graduate students, half are in these four fields.

There is no clear reason why national interest demands deferring an engineering graduate student, but not an American history student. The former may, upon completion of his studies, turn out to be a highway construction engineer, and the latter may become a schoolteacher. In my view, this will start the practice of draft dodging through graduate study all over again.

When the Senate accepted the Conference Report, we were told that, under the new law, it would no longer be possible to pyramid

57

The blame for this rampant inequality does not lie with those who take advantage of it, any more than we can blame those who legally use unfair tax loopholes. It lies with those of us in Congress and in the Administration who have failed to concern ourselves with the fairness of our Selective Service System. When the United States Senate debates the draft law for *two hours*—as it did in June 1967—we can hardly blame those young men who feel that the government does not care about their future.

Indeed, the Selective Service system sometimes sounds as though it welcomed the inequality of treatment, and the pressures the system induced. In a paper issued in June 1965 as part of the Selective Service orientation kit (and only recently withdrawn after pressure) the Selective Service expressed pride in its "channeling" of young men into "desirable" activities:

"The club of induction," said Selective Service, "has been used to drive out of areas considered to be less important to the areas of greater importance in which deferments were given, the individuals who did not or could not participate in activities which were considered essential to the defense of the Nation. . . . The psychology of granting wide choice under pressure to take action is the American or indirect way of achieving what is done by direction in foreign countries where choice is not permitted."

---

deferments, and thus to escape the draft altogether. Almost any college student can get a deferment. Then, if he chooses one of the deferable areas of study—engineering, mathematics, natural sciences, or health—his deferment is extended. When he finishes graduate school, if he chooses an occupation listed as critical or an activity listed as essential to the national interest, his deferment is once again extended. In short, he has beaten the draft.

The real effect of such pressure, of course, is to magnify inequality. Those with the money to extend their education; those with the educational background to gain technical skills; those who can support a family at an early age are all but exempt. Those who must work, those who cannot go to school, are drafted.

A PROGRAM FOR REFORM

I believe that drastic reforms are necessary. I proposed in the Congress last year a specific series of changes designed to improve the system. Most of these changes were defeated. But if adopted they will, I believe, minimize the interference which the military causes in young men's lives, while at the same time eliminating the inequalities which now infect the system.

These reforms have two elements: first, the drafting of men at an early age—when they reach nineteen; and second, the drastic curtailing of deferments, with the choice for service made on a random selection basis.

When a young man is nineteen, he is just starting his career of advanced education; he is probably not married; and he makes, according to the military, a better soldier than his elders. If the age of nineteen was the age for determining service, a youth would know early in life whether he would be called for service; and he would be spared the years of uncertainty which now cloud his life.

Further, since almost no nineteen-year-old is engaged in critical occupation, the entire structure of occupational deferments could be eliminated. While the system could still

59

take into account cases of extreme hardship—for example, where a youth was already the sole support of his family—there would be no need for the wide-ranging categories of activities "essential to the national interest" which local boards can apply or reject almost at will.

Moreover, college deferments—the single biggest source of economic discrimination in our draft system—would become irrelevant, at least in peacetime.[3] A youth in college at nineteen could finish his education, and then immediately be subject to random selection. If he chose to do so, of course, no deferment would be allowed, except in cases where induction would cause real hardship, as in the case of the sole surviving son or the only family breadwinner. All others would take their chances along with the nineteen-year-olds up for selection.

In addition to altering the pattern of occupational and educational deferments, we should also revise our medical and academic standards. Given an army where only a small minority actually face combat (fewer than half are in combat in Vietnam, and the fraction is far smaller if we compare men in combat to all those in the Armed Forces), there is no reason why men with asthma, or poor vision, or flat feet cannot be called. They can perform clerical, logistical, and support operations without any injury—and ought

[3] Under this system, I propose college deferments be abolished in wartime, but four-year college postponements be permitted in peacetime. For the purposes of this system I would define "wartime" as any period during which the number of American casualties resulting from armed conflict equalled or exceeded 10 percent of the number of persons being inducted into the military. In World War I, the ratio of casualties to inductees was 11 percent; in World War II, 11 percent; in Korea, 10 percent; in Vietnam so far, about 10.9 percent.

not to receive special treatment because of slight physical disabilities.

Similarly, we could increase the manpower pool by making an effort to use those who score low on the Armed Forces Qualification Test. The Defense Department has already succeeded in adapting some 100,000 "Group IV" men—those who scored low on the tests—to military service. Since many of those rejected *want* to serve in the Armed Forces, we could open military service to a group which can benefit by it as well as substantially assisting them in their later civilian life. At the same time, we could substantially lower the number of men we would have to draft.

Obviously objections can be made to these changes, particularly to the random selection method of choosing those who would enter the service. But if we understand that the "rational" national interest criteria have spawned unfair economic and racial distinctions, we can see why random selection is the most promising way of ending the abuses within the Selective Service System.[4]

Rather than being mindless or arbitrary, random selection would insure that every qualified young man would be equally liable to compulsory selective military service. It would erase the uncertainty now present and give the registrant a clear idea at the earliest possible time of whether or not he faces induction so he can plan his life accordingly. And it would eliminate the arbitrary distinctions which depend on the day of birth, the State's draft quota, the family's economic means, and the vagaries of local draft boards.

[4] A detailed description of my proposal system of Random Selection appears in the Appendix.

61

CONSCIENTIOUS OBJECTION

These changes in the structure of selective service will improve the draft. But a modern military system will also have to face a deeper objection raised by many of today's youth: their refusal to violate their individual consciences by participating in the draft. New York *Times* columnist James Reston estimated last year that, if student deferments were abolished, as many as one out of every four college students would refuse induction into the military. From my own discussions with students, I am convinced Mr. Reston is right. It is significant that many students are turning in their deferments, rejecting easy avoidance, and challenging the military on grounds of conscience. To many Americans, these students are misguided or even traitorous. I do not think their stand is that easily answered. Instead, it requires a look at the difficult question of conscientious objection.

The United States, along with most societies, has always understood that for some men, participation in war violates their deepest moral convictions. The Quakers, the Mennonites, the Amish—the traditional "peace" churches—have been allowed to place their members in non-combatant status, or in alternative service. The government thus recognizes that a democracy does not enjoy forcing individuals to violate their deep-rooted beliefs. As former Supreme Court Chief Justice Harlan F. Stone said in 1919, "It may well be questioned whether the state which preserves its life by a settled policy of steady violation of conscience of the individual will not in fact lose it by the process."

In the last fifty years, Congress has extended the right to claim CO status to all men who, "by religious training and belief," are conscientiously opposed to all forms of war. Even those who belonged to no church, in other words, would have their claims honored. And in 1965, the Supreme Court held in U.S. *v.* Seeger[5] that a man could be a CO even if he did not believe in God, as long as his pacifism was backed by deeply felt "religious beliefs."

Unfortunately, the Congress—probably reacting to the growing draft resistance movement—reversed this interpretation of the law in 1967. In my view this act was not only unwise but probably unconstitutional. A young man whose pattern of life indicates his moral opposition to all war should not be forced to violate his conscience because he does not believe in God. In fact, that is most likely a violation of the First Amendment's prohibition against religious discrimination. I would hope that the Congress will move swiftly to protect fully conscientious objectors.

A far more difficult question, but one which we must face, is the problem of those who are morally opposed to a particular war. From talking to many of these students, I am convinced that their opposition is based on moral grounds. They are hardly cowards; many have served in the Peace Corps, and risked death in the civil rights movement; many are willing to face a five-year jail term for their beliefs. Rather, as Governor Nelson A. Rockefeller's son Steven said some time ago, these objectors "are not

[5] 380 U.S. 163 (1965).

afraid to fight, but they are afraid to betray their consciences and unwilling to abandon their intelligence." When we add the consideration that the "just war" is a concept familiar in theology, we can see that it may well be possible to hold deep, religiously based, moral objections to particular wars.

Nonetheless, it would be extremely difficult to sort out moral from political objectors—or from those who simply did not wish to go into combat. It would require a detailed personal analysis of each youth, and a complex job of trying to separate out motives. To test sincerity for each objector to each war might create havoc in the administration of CO status. Moreover, selective conscientious objection might prove unfair to those who have not had the education to articulate their opposition to military service.

In peacetime, however, we could well accommodate those with moral objections to service in the military by greatly expanding alternative service. There are vitally needed tasks that must be done. Mental hospitals are short of orderlies; community development is still essential; police and firemen are desperately needed. If we developed a broad program of voluntary national service—for work in ghettos, on Indian reservations, in welfare agencies—and if we made service longer than the military, with less benefits, then those whose consciences are touched by the war might still be of use to the nation without participating in combat. Unless we are deliberately vindictive, there is no reason to punish men of conscience, and force them to go to jail, when they might be performing useful national service at no cost to their own moral codes. In addition, we could link alternative service in peacetime to the lottery. We could let youths choose other service—again, for longer periods at less pay—and let them define for themselves the work they can do to make this a better nation.

I, for one, do not accept the belief that a man owes nothing to his country. But I also reject the notion that we should run roughshod over the consciences of our citizens, or rest content with an unfair and arbitrary system. When we ask one young man to risk his life for his country, and tell another his life can proceed undisturbed, we must be sure we have devised the fairest way humanly possible to choose between them. We must be sure we have allowed every young man as much flexibility as our military needs permit in making his personal choice as to the quality and kind of service he is asked to give his nation.

DISSENTING YOUTH: THE
DANGER AND THE PROMISE

We will face in the coming decade a larger and more articulate student generation, committed to participation in the political life of America, and willing to dissent from conditions which they regard as unjust or immoral. Without a clear understanding of what dissent means in a democracy, their energy and insight will be lost to us. Disturbingly, this has already begun.

On October 21, 1967, somewhere between 50,000 and 100,000 Americans rallied at the Lincoln Memorial to oppose the conduct of the war in Vietnam. There were speeches, placards, songs of protest—traditional expressions of disagreement with public policy. What followed was different. Thousands of the demonstrators marched across Washington's Memorial Bridge to the Pentagon. There, a small minority camped for two days and nights. Some tried to storm the Pentagon; others sat, refusing to move. Many were injured; hundreds were arrested.

This "confrontation," and the division between the traditional protestors and those who were determined to "confront the warmakers," was a disturbing symbol of developing trends among our dissenting youth. It was disturbing not because of "Communist influence" but because of what it may portend. We are facing, I am afraid, a significant trend away from democratic dissent, toward new, divisive, and potentially disastrous tactics which will harm the demonstrators and their cause, and could well impair our framework of political liberty.

The threat posed by the tactic of disruption is more than a disturbance of the peace; it is a threat to the invaluable contribution that the disaffected youth have made to their country, and to ourselves. Over the last seven years, we have seen emerge a generation, mostly among the educated, the affluent, and the most intelligent, committed to making the ideals of democracy a reality. They have risked their careers, their safety, their comfort, and their lives to put their principles into action. I think they have made us a better people for it.

It was not long ago that professors and commentators were deploring the "Silent Generation" of the 1950s—a collection of students who accepted the values they were taught, and who were content to live out their lives in the categories assigned to them; working for the corporation, the law firm, the university, accepting the material benefits of affluence and not looking beyond their own personal lives. Protest was almost unheard of. The poet Karl Shapiro wrote in 1957, "Passivity is the last word we expect to use in connection with a generation of students, but that's the only word that applies to the American university of the last few years." They were being trained to serve; and they learned their lesson well. In an ironically serene prediction, the University of California's president, Clark Kerr, prophesied in 1959:

"The employers will love this generation. They aren't going to press many grievances. They are going to be easy to handle. There aren't going to be any riots."

Looking out over the 8000 students boycotting classes at Berkeley five years later, President Kerr might have wondered what had happened.

What had happened was that American youth—at least, that minority that cared about the injustices yet to be overcome—found the strength to dramatize those injustices, and the courage to fight for change. If we would understand what has driven many of our young people to extreme forms of protest, we must look back at why the young generation of today has become the most active and visible one in our history; and why they have become so disillusioned with the prospects for reform that some have embraced disruptive revolution.

THE ROOTS OF INVOLVEMENT

Until the Second World War, college was a place for a small minority of Americans. In 1940, some 1,500,000 students attended college—less than a third of the college-age population. These students tended to be from the wealthier segments of society, secure in the knowledge they could expect to hold a high place in the nation's economic and social life. And those that did have to work their way through college were far too busy trying to stay alive and maintain their jobs and their grades in class to concern themselves with other affairs. Despite the flurry of student activism in the 1930s, college still was, in the main, a place of serenity, a preparation for a life of earning.

By 1960, this had changed. The college population had exploded as the nation's growing affluence and its increased commitment to higher education opened the doors to qualified youngsters. College became the norm, not the exception. Some 6,500,000 students are now in college and soon the majority of American youth will have a college education. In addition, those in college were products of an affluent age, a time that had never known economic catastrophe, and a time of rapid communication and mobilization. It was a time when a nationwide student community became a reality; and without the threat of joblessness and poverty, this community could afford to become involved with other, broader concerns. The time was ripe for an issue. In 1960, that issue surfaced.

In one sense, this active generation of dissenting youths can pinpoint its birth: it was February 1, 1960. On that day, four freshmen from the all-Negro North Carolina Agricultural and Technical College in Greensboro sat down at a Woolworth's lunch counter and requested service. They were refused; but they stayed. And they set in motion the fusion of college students with public political issues that still continues.

The sit-in at Greensboro, and those that followed across the South, were certainly not the first examples of direct

69

action in the cause of civil rights. The NAACP and CORE had sponsored "sit-ins" in Chicago in the late 1940s; and Dr. Martin Luther King had organized the Montgomery bus boycott four years earlier. Two youth marches for integrated schools had taken place in Washington in 1957 and 1959, although few people noticed them.

But in early 1960, a college generation looked South, and found people their own age risking injury and death to protest a clear case of injustice. They began to react. My college generation probably would have shrugged its shoulders and gone back to looking at the football schedule. But in Northern schools—from New York through Wisconsin and Michigan, and out to California—students began to identify with the young Negroes sitting in. Chain stores were picketed, funds were raised, and thousands of students demonstrated their sympathy.

This was still a modest beginning, but it grew. With the Freedom Rides of 1961, young people actually ventured to the deep South, and saw instances of brutality and prejudice firsthand. The following summers they returned in force to organize Negroes, to teach children—and again, to face an entrenched system that was unwilling to yield, and the violent fringe of that system which engineered such brutal acts as the murders in 1964 of Andrew Goodman, James Chaney, and Michael Schwerner.

I dwell on this civil rights experience because it is important in understanding the tenor of dissent. There were other issues—nuclear testing and disarmament foremost among them—but civil rights was the key issue in which students were involved. These students came back from the South with several firmly established premises. First, theirs was primarily a *moral* cause; they felt far more sharply than their elders the overwhelming inhumanity of denying people a chance for a decent life because of the color of their skin. And they came back from the Alabama and Mississippi experiences shaken by contacts with those who wanted to preserve this inhumanity. They saw civic leaders and public officials defend segregation, and wink at acts of physical terror. They had seen firsthand that authority and justice were not always the same thing.

Thus, when these students came back to their campuses, they had learned to think about their elders—their leaders —as something to be fought, to be overcome. This was a lesson many took to heart when they began protesting their *own* treatment as students. If you could demonstrate, picket, and rally against conservative segregationists, why not use the same tactics against a college administration denying free expression?

The disaffected young did just that—most spectacularly at Berkeley, but also at Yale, at St. John's in New York City, and other campuses. Student strikes, boycotts and protests became commonplace on campuses, in support of their civil rights. And the "enemy" was no longer Southern segregation, but liberal college administrators, who had fought the hardest for academic freedom, and against loyalty oaths and McCarthyism a few years back.

While the battlefield was different from the South, the same principle was at stake, in the eyes of the students: the right to participate in democratic society. The case for direct, dramatic action was becoming extended.[1]

[1] One student leader, comparing Berkeley and Mississippi, put it this way: "The two battlefields may seem quite different to some

But the final and most drastic cause of protest escalation has been the war in Vietnam. Again, these students do not think primarily in terms of power politics or international law. They do not root for Ho Chi Minh or the Viet Cong; rather, they see in the war the participation of the total American system in an immoral action. For here, a policy endorsed by many members of the traditional liberal community, backed by the majority of the American people and their representatives, is, in their eyes, causing the death of thousands of innocent people for an unjustifiable purpose. It is this focus—on the human side of the war which we of other generations too rarely debate—that has divided so many of our young men and women from us.

Thus the equation is completed. If it is legitimate to disrupt a racist society, if it is permissible to interrupt the process of education to win civil liberty, then it must also be morally right to disrupt the process of an entire nation, if that nation is committing immoral acts abroad. At Berkeley in 1964, Free Speech Movement leader Mario Savio told a rally:

"There is a time when the operation of the machine becomes so odious, makes you so sick at heart that you can't take part; you can't even tacitly take part, and you've got to put your bodies upon the levers, upon all the apparatus, and you've got to make it stop."

This, in its extreme form, is what the student protests have bred. Among a small minority of dissenters, the goal now is not to persuade America to change its Vietnam

observers, but this is not the case. The same rights are at stake in both places—the right to participate as citizens in democratic society, and the right to due process of law."

policy, but to disrupt the American process. This is not inference—it is an avowed goal of some. The slogan of the 1967 Pentagon march was: "From Dissent to Resistance"; it has been seen in numerous attempts on dozens of colleagues to prevent those representing pro-war positions from speaking, or carrying out recruitment activities.[2] Those who advocate disruption do not deny their intention. They avow their lack of concern for the rights of others. "The government," said one student, "has abandoned its right of free speech. They have no more right to speak than a storm trooper in Nazi Germany." At Columbia University, a leader of a "resistance" movement asserted that ending the war was far more important than "abiding by the traditional rules" and more important than "an orderly America."

THE CASE AGAINST DISRUPTION

This argument must be examined with great care, for it has both hidden flaws and obvious dangers. In the first place, it is not even an appropriate part of civil disobedience. That course, exemplified by Thoreau's refusal to pay taxes in protest against the Mexican War of 1848 (for which he was jailed), is to decline to obey a law, as a means of making a personal moral stand. In the words of

[2] I was a victim of one such manifestation at the University of Wisconsin in the spring of 1966. Although my position on the war was not unsympathetic to theirs, a small minority of the audience kept the hall in a turmoil, and kept me from speaking for 1½ hours. (Shortly afterward, 4000 students at the university sent me a petition of apology.)

Catholic theologian John Cogley, who advocates civil disobedience, it means "to resist evil, to refuse to cooperate with evildoing, to do all in one's power to persuade others that the evil they see *is* evil." But it does not mean violent disruption of the conduct of others. As Cogley says, "those opposed to the Vietnam war have no right to destroy law and order at home, or to practice sedition or sabotage." And Paul Goodman, long an eloquent dissenter says, "I cannot accept the *putschist* use of violence. This is unacceptable, not because it is a fantasy—in a complex technology a few clever people can make a shambles—but because out of the shambles can come only the same bad world."

Thoreau did not pay his taxes; but neither did he stop troops bound for Mexico, or shout down those who favored that war. Disruption is a strange way to protest the use of force to settle disputes.[8]

Secondly, it is not in keeping with the intellectual tradition of a student generation. Dissent should express more than a crude emotionalism; slogans on buttons are no substitute for knowledge of issues. As Justice Oliver Wendell Holmes once said, the true test of a liberal mind is its passion for the facts. And more than any other Americans, students have the opportunity to meet this test. They have the time and mental energy, the freedom from the pressures and obligations of holding a job and raising a family. They

[8] Even the radical students, at least a few years ago, understood the danger of using immoral means to win desired ends. The Port Huron statement, founding statement of the Students for a Democratic Society, argues that "ends and means are intimately related . . . vague appeals to posterity cannot justify the mutilation of the present."

74

can examine society's defects critically and expose them temperately.

Further, the blunt truth is that the shock tactics of resistance will not work. The confrontation at the Pentagon and the blocking of the induction centers last fall did more than anything else to stem temporarily what had been a rising tide of criticism of the war. Those who bear peaceful witness for their convictions stir the American conscience. Those who call for violence and destruction offend it. Those who canvassed door to door to seek out people sincerely troubled by the war have won converts and strengthened their cause. Those who have burned their draft cards and our flag have scared them off.

This "backlash" is rooted in reason; for violence is repugnant to the better instincts of all our people, the very instincts the dissenters appeal to in their case against the war. Indeed, dissenters who stress the morality of acts should ask themselves what kind of ethic they breed. If any group in America with a deeply felt conviction should use disruption, what kind of a nation would we have? Shall we have anti-UN forces blocking General Assembly meetings? Or Southern sheriffs assaulting voting registrars?

Finally, these dissenters should ask what sort of long run results they will achieve. The most probable result will be that the tactics used by some will make genuine dissent more difficult, jeopardizing the right to speak that so far has been preserved. Until now, the New Left, unlike segments of the extreme right, has not resorted to force to attain its objectives. To do so now would pose a severe threat to its survival. The first sentence of the Constitution assigned to the government the task to "insure domestic tranquillity." At the same time, the Bill of Rights safeguards free speech. The balance thus struck is in favor of peaceful exercise of this right. When those who oppose government policies cross the line between dissent and the use of muscle, they risk creating a reaction that will destroy all that has been done to preserve speech and dissent in our country.

There are some young people who admit these pitfalls, but argue that nothing else will work. They have petitioned peacefully, and argued for their cause, and yet the war machine, in their eyes, goes on as if they did not exist. I would urge them to look carefully at American history before concluding that our process of reform and peaceful debate is not worth saving. Fifty years ago it seemed to many that this nation was totally hostile to the rights of labor. Courts issued injunctions barring strikes; anti-trust laws were used to break up unions. But within a few years, the Wagner Act guaranteed labor's rights; and a new Supreme Court gave labor full protection to organize. Ten years ago a poor man had neither a lawyer nor anything like equal justice. Today, we have seen a revolution in criminal justice: bail, counsel, constitutional rights are now available to men of all economic backgrounds. And, within a decade, the federal government has changed from an indifferent observer of the racial struggle to a full-blooded advocate of racial equality.

THE LESSONS OF HISTORY

Change does not, of course, come smoothly. We need protest to highlight the wrongs which exist, and the need to right them. But this government *can* change. It is no monolith—it is a set of different men and different interests, many who have entered government because they believe the world needs changing.

Those who think they have been "powerless" confuse influence with total victory. Our country is full of influential interest groups—farmers, miners, conservationists, rifle associations—advocating strong views on public issues, frustrated because they want much more than they can get. (Even the magazines of the military reserve associations, ever since I can remember, have bemoaned the fact that their domestic foes were winning, that the arms buildup was lagging.) Our system works through the tugging and hauling, the conflict of groups with strong views, and the eventual mediation of the conflict by elected representatives.

No group gets everything it wants. But even the lessening of what one considers an evil can be taken as a victory if it is viewed with reason and perspective. And I have no doubt that the poverty program is less hobbled, the Negro less oppressed, and the effort to control nuclear warfare more successful because of the effect of peaceful dissent over the last few years. This is far from Utopia, but it is an important contribution to the politics of the Sixties.

I have stressed the danger of extremism in dissent. But the American people should not permit the most dra-

77

matic forms of protest to blind them to the peaceful dissent taking place. The "teach-ins" on Vietnam; the door-to-door campaigns to organize opposition; the running of dissenting candidates in primaries—all these efforts have resulted in by far the greatest debate about a war, during wartime, that we have ever had. In a large measure, it is the academic community which has kept a curtain of silence from suppressing debate about this tragic war; it is the young people who have shown us that we are strong enough to dispute even the acts of a government during war, and that is a profound demonstration of our national strength. To call these dissenters "traitors" or "Communists" is wrong and dangerously irresponsible. Their protest is rooted in a belief that the United States is betraying rather than honoring its principles. It may be politically helpful for public officials to strike a heroic pose against a dissident minority, but it will not help to restore the dialogue we so badly need in America.

Nor does it help to allege that such protests encourage the enemy to prolong the war. With this argument, no protest against a misguided foreign policy would be permissible. Once our government took action, we would all be required to assent. This is not part of either the letter or spirit of the Constitution, and it is a profoundly short-sighted view. Any enemy who looks at our country will quickly realize that we can have far-reaching internal debate and still defend our vital interests. Indeed, such debate is one of the interests we seek to defend, for ourselves and the nations we protect.

My hope, therefore, is not that protest will cease, but

78

that it will remember the purpose of dissent from official policy. To be effective—to be useful—protest must reach those with the power to change things. It must touch the conscience of Americans. And it must be protest with alternatives. We know that our youth today is more than a generation in protest; they want, more genuinely and thoroughly than any other, to help change the world. The Peace Corps, VISTA, tutorial programs, community action projects—these successes have won for our youth the right to be listened to, and the right to be taken seriously. Hopefully, this right will not be lost by an inaccurate and dangerous belief that our system cannot absorb change and new ideas. It can—it must—it needs them to survive. But it will not have them if some of the best of our young minds conclude that the structure is not worth the effort it will take to make it strong. And it will not have them if the older generation does not understand that each age is unique, with its own perspectives and its own priorities. If the young dissent, it is from what we, through our acts and our indifference, allowed to happen. They may not be realistic or polite, but their basic idealism and purpose are inescapable. They are, in a sense, our conscience—annoying, disturbing, but necessary to have with us. They are telling us things we may not want to hear, but which we ought to know. They are forcing us, as a nation, to face the promise of our heritage, and its reality.

The Persian poet, Kahlil Gibran, once said to parents about their children:

> You may give them your love but not your
> thoughts, for they have their own thoughts.

79

You may house their bodies but not their souls,
    for their souls dwell in the house of tomorrow,
    which you cannot visit, not even in your dreams.

You may strive to be like them, but seek not
    to make them like you.

For life goes not backward nor tarries with yesterday.

You are the bows from which your children as living
    arrows are sent forth.

They are different; many are angry. But if they can become part of our society, and not be estranged from it, we will all be the better for it.

THE FIRST DUTY OF GOVERN-MENT—THE CONTROL OF CRIME

No human need is more basic than personal security. No freedom is more instinctive than freedom from fear. If we are not safe in our homes and on our streets, if we are threatened—whether by an agent of a police state or by a single criminal—then we are not free. The first duty of government, as Thomas Hobbes observed in the seventeenth century, is to provide that protection which is the root of freedom and security.

Today, this first duty has been made more difficult by the rising rate of crime and violence in our nation. This is more than a crisis in itself. A pervasive crime problem is a barrier to progress elsewhere. A nation obsessed with crime cannot apply itself to the tasks of providing adequate jobs, housing and health for its citizens. Moreover, we cannot survive as a community if our attitude toward fellow citizens is scarred by the insistent fear of violent attack.

Crime in America has traditionally been a state and local matter—largely because we have always feared the creation of a centralized state with a national police. But crime today is a matter of national debate because it is a national crisis. The rate of crime has almost tripled since 1940; and rates are now increasing six times faster than our population. Between 1960 and 1964, an average of about 3,000,000 crimes were committed each year. In 1965, that figure jumped more than 22 percent. The dollar cost of this criminal activity is close to $21,000,000,000 a year; and even if we subtract the costs of "crimes without victims"—largely gambling—the expense of criminal activity is astronomical. The cost in human terms—to the victim and to his family, to the criminal and society—is so staggering it cannot be measured.

These figures are, regrettably, not misleading. They do not disguise trivial offenses of little damage. Homicides in 1965 increased 19 percent over the preceding five year average; forcible rapes increased 31.5 percent; 22.4 percent more robberies were committed, and the one year rise in aggravated assaults was 26.8 percent. We see, then, not simply an increase in illegality, but an alarming rise in violent attacks on innocent persons.

It is depressing to catalog crime as a major problem for the 1970s. But every indication is that the crime dilemma will get worse; for it is among youth that criminal offenses are increasing most sharply. Of the 5,000,000 arrests made in 1965, the largest single group—more than 1,000,000—were those under eighteen. Taken as a group, people under twenty-four accounted for more than 40 percent of all those arrested—including more than 40 percent of robbery arrests and 70 percent of rape arrests. When we realize that the highest rate of arrest occurs among those fifteen to seventeen years old, we glimpse a grim picture of the prospects for a lawful, orderly society in the 1970s.

The growth of crime in the United States has produced damaging reactions. Abroad, it has become fashionable to brand America as a land of violence, drawing a national pattern out of the "Wild West" image of our past, the era of gang warfare, and today's riots in our cities. This Hollywood image, blind to our history of resolving our most searing internal disputes in our courts and legislatures, can only gain currency as the level of violence in American life continues. Indeed, some noted literary minds in the United States are turning to this image, as an explanation for everything from our social customs to our foreign policy.

Far more serious is the reaction of our own citizens to crime. We seem to be willing to accept the growth of lawlessness, even as we become frightened by it to the point of obsession. Many retreat from society, doubling the locks on their doors, not daring to venture out at night. Forty-three percent of the citizens in one major city, says President Johnson's Crime Commission Report, are afraid to walk the streets at night because of fear of crime. Our citizens urge that more police be hired; ultimately, they move out of neighborhoods that are centers of crime. These are all natural reactions; but they are essentially futile. Crime, for one thing, is not confined to any area—in the affluent "safe" suburbs serious crime is now 50 percent more frequent than in rural areas, and fully 60 percent of the

83

rate in large cities. Moreover, a nation of cities locked in fear is not an answer to crime—it is surrender to it.

ARE THE COURTS THE CAUSE?

Some—perhaps by now a majority of Americans—will claim that the answer to our crime problem lies in "getting tough" with criminal suspects, returning to the freewheeling days when police methods were wholly outside the realm of judicial supervision. There is widespread belief that "courts are coddling criminals" and that the "rights of the individual are destroying the rights of society." These views, prevalent as they are, are mistaken and dangerous. They are mistaken because they misconceive the relation between individual liberty and crime; they are dangerous because they threaten vital constitutional rights without providing any real answer to the growth of crime.

The most hotly debated issue concerns the protection given to persons suspected of having committed crimes. Through a series of Supreme Court decisions, we have made it a constitutional obligation for police to arrest suspects only on "probable cause"; search suspects and their dwellings only within narrow limits; and—in the controversial *Escobedo*[1] and *Miranda*[2] cases—inform every person arrested of his right to remain silent and to consult an attorney before being questioned by police.

The root complaint—voiced by such prominent citizens as former Vice-President Richard M. Nixon—is that these

[1] Escobedo *v.* Illinois 378 U.S. 478 (1964).
[2] Miranda *v.* Arizona 384 U.S. 436 (1966).

84

decisions "have weakened the law and encouraged the criminal, weakened the peace forces as against the criminal forces." This is a serious charge, but it is also very doubtful. In the first place, the effect of these decisions on police questioning appears to be almost non-existent. The *Yale Law Journal,* in an exhaustive study of police questioning before and after the *Miranda* case found almost no effect. Suspects that wanted to talk did so after knowing their rights. Considering that the overwhelming majority of suspects plead guilty, confessing despite knowledge of their rights, the *Miranda* case loses much of its threat. The results tend to support the claim by Nathan Sobeloff, a prominent New York jurist, that confessions are a vastly overrated part of the criminal process.

Indeed, these decisions could, in the long run, help the fight against crime. The abuse of suspects in police stations has probably created more criminals than any court decision. It has taught people, particularly in poverty neighborhoods, that the police, their methods, and ultimately the law itself are hostile to them. Moreover, many police chiefs acknowledge that these decisions have prodded them into using more modern and effective methods to produce evidence. Thus, the cases they bring into court are based on more solid evidence than in the past.

More fundamentally, these decisions did *not* create any new right to remain silent. This has long been a basic privilege of suspects—otherwise, police would be free to badger suspects until their will was exhausted. (There have been enough false confessions to warn us of the grave danger of erasing the privileges of silence and consultation with an attorney.) The only really new holding was that sus-

85

pects must be *told* of their constitutional rights, and that poor defendants must be provided with attorneys. These holdings, it seems to me, are matters of basic fairness. It is indefensible to deprive a man of a clear constitutional protection, simply because he doesn't know what his rights are.

To make the availability of the advice of an attorney depend on the wealth of a citizen flies in the face of our promise of "equal justice under law." Ignorance of the law may be no excuse for an illegal act; but it is also no excuse for stripping a man of his rights. Further, such conduct does not harm the "hardened criminal"; he is fully aware of his defense. It is, instead, the "first-timer"—the uneducated, the frightened, and in some cases, the innocent suspect—who suffers most from his ignorance.

It may be true that these rights only help the "obviously guilty" or the "undesirables"; police, after all, rarely arrest an affluent, respectable citizen for questioning. But we should remember, as Supreme Court Justice Felix Frankfurter once observed, that "the safeguards of liberty have frequently been forged in controversies involving not very nice people." And if we deprive "undesirables" of their rights, we may soon find ourselves the victims of our indifference. A society where police can stop, search and question any of its people at will has sacrificed an important personal right—the right to be let alone—for the illusion of security.

We need police forces which vigorously combat crime, and most of them do. But we also need police who honor the rights of all citizens. I can understand why police do not like to be deprived of any tool of law enforcement.

This complaint, however, has been made ever since the Supreme Court first threw out a state court confession thirty years ago—a confession obtained by beating suspects for several hours with studded belts.[8]

We dare not meet the problem of crime by turning our backs on the Constitution. A democracy always takes a risk—for it assumes that we can and must fight law-breakers in a lawful manner. But it is the only sensible way for a free society to behave. As Supreme Court Justice Louis D. Brandeis said, we will not win respect for law if we permit those who enforce it to behave in a lawless manner.

So crime will not be controlled by abandoning criminal safeguards. It will be controlled instead by giving to the police the best weapons of crime detection and control we can fashion—and by making new efforts to meet the social causes of crime.

It is an anomaly that the United States—the most technically advanced society in history—continues to rely on outmoded and cumbersome methods of crime prevention and detection. Patrolmen walk the beat; patrol cars cruise high-crime areas; police headquarters learn about crimes only by haphazard reporting of victims and witnesses—if they bother to take the time. The astonishing fact is that we have largely failed to put our awesome technical skill to work on the problem of crime control.

Some technical possibilities are extremely simple. Many apartment buildings in large cities, for example, have flashing lights outside to call taxicabs. It would be simple to link up a similar system at apartment entrances and lobbies,

[8] Brown _v._ Mississippi—U.S.—1935.

summoning cruising police immediately to the scene of trouble. Similarly, telephones exist in almost every American home. Surely a communications network which can flash television signals around the world can devise a single number to alert the police to trouble at any address.

The technical world offers, in addition, far more sophisticated possibilities. Recording devices are now being developed which can identify people by "voiceprints"—as distinctive as fingerprints and far more difficult to disguise. It may soon be possible to mark valuable property with very small-yield radioactive isotopes, providing far more positive means of identification, and seriously hampering the underworld network of "fences," who dispose of stolen goods.

In addition, the computer offers rich promise in the improvement of police work. We are just beginning to utilize the whole field of "information retrieval"—identifying fingerprints, cataloging automated information, sorting out data on wanted persons and stolen property. The widespread use of the computer—linked to machines across the country—would provide effective aids to investigation.

The computer can also provide sophisticated, detailed information on crime patterns. Rather than relying on guesswork or laborious charting of criminal activity, computers can diagnose—in seconds—particular patterns of crime, and can aid in the deployment of police. Chicago has already experimented in this way, and crime in that city has dropped in the face of a national increase.

HOW TO SUPPORT THE POLICE

Police can also be assisted by the use of new planning techniques. The Planning Program Budget System—"PPBS" —has worked with great success in the Department of Defense in properly allocating costs and effort. New York City is already experimenting with its use in the police department; and it offers a promising method of reducing waste and inefficiency in this vital area.

It is clear, however, that if we are to modernize police weapons, we must modernize the police departments themselves. All these techniques, all our resources, depend ultimately on the individual police forces across the nation. It is the policeman who stands between the criminal and the law-abiding citizen. And it can be the policeman who also stands between a youth and a life of crime.

I have a great deal of respect for the work of the police; but the police today are burdened and we must recognize that in large measure the burden comes from public indifference. We want police to catch criminals, and protect our lives, safety, and property. But we do not seem willing to give them the tools and the money they need. We seem to want them to use all methods—however brutal and unconstitutional—to deal with suspects, but we are unwilling to give them the minimal cooperation they need to do their job effectively.

In addition, municipal governments have for too long neglected police organization. Cities and towns next door to one another resist consolidating their efforts and pooling

89

their detective services, despite the fact that criminals can easily cross city lines. Traditionally, the police force has been the way by which men from poor families have been able to make a secure career, while they served their communities. But in many large cities, police forces have tended toward clannishness. Promotion has been by seniority, bringing to the top men whose orientation is toward a former day when law enforcement was much simpler. In addition, police forces have tended to exclude newer groups of the poor. In New York City, Negroes and Puerto Ricans make up almost 30 percent of the population—but less than 8 percent of the police are Negroes and Puerto Ricans. The spectre of white police patrolling Negro districts—especially where the police exhibit clear signs of contempt for minorities—has been a prime source of racial tension in our large communities. It is no accident in almost every one of our major urban race riots over the past four years—Harlem in 1964, Watts in 1965, Newark and Detroit in 1967—the spark that set the trouble off was the arrest of a Negro by white police.

There is a simple key step that can be taken to improve the quality and performance of our police: to bring new kinds of citizens into the departments; from the low-income ghetto groups, from the universities and from the technological fields. Recruitment of ghetto youth would be more than a social gesture. Fused with new police approaches, it would help curb crime as well. A citizenry which respects its police cooperates with them; and it is clear that, in ghetto areas, it is not so much *police* who are resented, but the way police operate. The poor—those with incomes below $3000—are the principal victims of crime; and most crime occurs in poor areas. They want police protection desperately, but they want it without the casual brutality and abuse that characterizes many police-community relations. If we make an effort—through support during training periods, and with a more flexible promotion system—to bring new groups into our police forces, we may take a major step forward in improving their work.

President Johnson's Crime Commission has suggested the use of "community service officers"—hired from the diverse neighborhoods of the city—to act as unarmed apprentice police, bridging the gap between community and police. The success of Tampa's use of 120 men in this area was a prime reason why violence was tempered in that city last summer.[4] Similarly, police work ought to be a prime field for college graduates. At a time when almost half of our young men go to college, very few college graduates go into police work. This is indeed unfortunate, since few avenues of public service offer more responsibility and more potential for the individual to help his community in a meaningful and satisfying way. The policeman, after all, is a combination lawyer, prosecutor, and judge. He is as well a protector of the public, a mediator of disputes, and an example to youth. Surely his profession should be one which appeals to the educated and dedicated young man.

Police forces need more technically trained personnel.

[4] During the Senate Judiciary Committee's hearings on the riot control bill in the summer of 1967, to offer a more balanced view on the question, Senator Hugh Scott of Pennsylvania and I arranged for one of the Tampa "white hats" to testify on how his group operated in the Negro community. I commend his testimony to cities seeking the best way to prevent such disturbances. See testimony of Norris Morrow, *Hearings before the Senate Committee on the Judiciary, on H.R. 421*, Pt. 2, pp. 680–98.

The whole area of research and development is flourishing; more than 200,000 scientists and engineers work in defense-related fields alone. Clearly this talent must become an integral part of police work in the 1970s. New techniques, new organizational methods, can turn our police forces from dedicated but handicapped, into fully effective crime-fighting units. Here again the President's Crime Commission has offered a valuable suggestion—recruitment of technical experts as "police-agents" to work in fields like ballistics and computer management without long apprenticeship on the beat or in the station house.

These changes will require money. We now spend more than $3,000,000,000 each year on police protection; yet the average patrolman in our largest cities—where crime is most serious—receives only $7000 a year. This, in turn, forces police to moonlight to support the family instead of using that time to gain technical skills, and a better understanding of the social roots of crime.

I believe urgent financial improvement is necessary. We must raise the salaries of police; we must provide benefits commensurate with the risk they run, such as a double-indemnity life-insurance program similar to that provided federal government employees. (I have introduced legislation to this effect in the Senate.) Further, credits should be awarded for police who take advanced work in police skills. At the same time, policemen have to be freed from the burden of forms, paperwork, and mechanical details which keep them in the station house and out of the crime areas. This very need, however, holds out promise. If we could recruit citizens from all parts of the community to act as clerical help in police stations, it would at once accomplish three important goals—diversifying the makeup of police departments, providing employment for needy citizens, and liberating the police from paperwork.

Finally, we can improve crime-fighting techniques by giving the police new methods of subduing suspects. At present, police carry with them clumsy weapons—the billyclub and the gun—which are either useless or lethal. It is inexcusable to force a policeman either to let a fleeing criminal go, or else risk killing him. A variety of more sophisticated weapons exist to provide more reasonable alternatives—chemical sprays, "tranquilizing" guns, sprays which mark suspects for capture by other police—all these are weapons which can be effective, without causing the human tragedies of needless injury or death.

CONTROL OF FIREARMS

But if we are to discourage the official use of firearms, it is even more vital to prevent the use of guns by the lawless and the irresponsible. The indiscriminate use of firearms in this nation is something close to barbarism. Every two minutes someone in America is killed, wounded, or maimed by a firearm. The prime source for this carnage is the indiscriminate sale of weapons without control and regulation. In addition to the wide-open sale of guns in stores, thousands of weapons are shipped each year through the mail, with no questions asked, sold for less than the cost of a pair of shoes. Over a recent three-year period in Chicago, four thousand people bought weapons from

93

two mail-order dealers; one thousand of them had criminal records.

Each state has the power to determine the use of, the sale and the possession of arms by its own citizens. If a state like Idaho, because of the popularity of hunting, wants minimum gun-control laws, that is up to the people of Idaho. But those states with pressing crime problems should not be frustrated in their efforts by an indiscriminate sale of guns across state lines. My own state of Massachusetts, for example, has stringent gun-control laws. But we have a serious firearms problem nonetheless; 87 percent of the concealed firearms used in Massachusetts crimes come from out of state. We cannot cope with the problem by ourselves.

What we and other states need is an effective law regulating the interstate flow of guns. Such a law would in no way impair the legitimate use of guns for recreation. But it would control the interstate movement of firearms, to protect states that wish to enforce their own firearms laws. Up to now, a powerful and vocal lobby has stifled effective federal gun-control laws. But I cannot believe that our people will tolerate another decade of senseless, wanton misuse of weapons which causes thousands of deaths and injuries each year.

AGAINST THE REAL CAUSES OF CRIME

The changes I have outlined would give us a far more effective program to fight crime. But we also must make efforts to combat the long-range causes of crime. In part, this means vigorous efforts to reach those outside the mainstream of American social life. A community at work rebuilding itself, and giving new hope to its citizens, is not likely to either tolerate or breed criminals—even if it engaged in sharp political fights. (Indeed, those who confidently assert that direct political action breeds "disrespect for the law" should look more closely at the facts. In Montgomery, Alabama, at the height of civil rights demonstrations, the Negro crime rate declined to almost zero.) But this work, however vigorous, cannot in the short run aid those who have already turned to crime. It is in this field that we have failed most appallingly in applying workable techniques to the crime problem. And it is here that the 1970s will hopefully see substantial progress.

At present, the rehabilitation of criminals is an idea honored in rhetoric and neglected in practice. We spend more than one billion dollars each year in administering our prison system, with its population of more than 200,000. Ostensibly, our prisons are designed to "rehabilitate"—to prepare the prisoner for return to civilian life.

The majority of states run correctional systems which do not correct; they simply hold prisoners, without the staff or the equipment to rehabilitate them. Thus our jails have become, in the words of Attorney General Ramsey Clark, "temporary cell blocks which prepare inmates for further crime." More than 50 percent of the men in jail today will go on to commit more crimes, adding to the mounting police, correctional, and human costs, further ruining their own lives and the life of society. This is

95

wholly irrational. Once we have men in the custody of the state, it is simply self-defeating not to do all in our power to turn these inmates away from the practice of crime.

The function of criminal correction must be to apprehend the criminal, to deal with him as an individual, to teach him the skills of a trade or profession, so he can return to his community as a useful citizen. No effort will wholly succeed; but it can turn thousands of criminals into participating citizens.

Here again, our society has suffered from a failure of perception. We understand the menace of crime; and we want the largest police forces possible to prevent it. But we have not been willing to spend funds to turn criminals into contributors. Several states, in fact, have developed promising plans for revamping their corrections systems; but they do not have the money to put these plans into operation. It should be a matter of high priority for state and local officials to press for proper funds for these programs.

We should also greatly expand the present number of probation and parole officers. These officers have such heavy caseloads that they cannot possibly give each offender the time and individual attention he needs to make his readjustment to society successfully. The money involved in changing this will help buy a system which can save these men from further crime and lead them to a normal life. Probation and parole work—involving as it does the chance to literally salvage a life—could also be a rewarding career for young people. Coupled with a program of federal grants for innovative corrections programs, these funds can help salvage the lives of many human beings, and help avoid the consequences of further crime.

Further, we should adopt programs that have worked successfully elsewhere. Some federal prisons have begun work release programs, where prisoners work in the community by day, earning money and job skills, and return to the prison at night. State prisons in Wisconsin and North Carolina have pioneered new types of rehabilitation and release techniques. In California, a wide range of experimental programs have been started, including "prisons" without cells or walls, and job training programs run by local businessmen.

No criminal rehabilitation program can succeed without a major effort against drug addiction. In cities like New York, almost half the criminal offenses are committed by addicts, desperate for funds to support their habit. These people cannot be treated as criminals; prison terms cannot cure them. If we do not make a full effort to eliminate addiction among our criminals, they will only return to addicton—and crime—as soon as they are released.

Here we have encouraging guideposts. Congress in 1966 passed a small-scale pilot program under which addicts charged with or convicted of federal offenses can be civilly committed—not imprisoned—if it is found they can benefit from medical treatment. If they respond to treatment, they are then returned to their communities under carefully supervised conditions, including job placement, and continuing medical and psychiatric treatment. California has found that about half of those committed have been able to lead lives without addiction. This work, pioneered by the President's Committee on Narcotics and the Narcotics Addict Rehabilitation Act of 1966,[5] should be accelerated. With the proper effort in building adequate treatment facilities, it may be possible to employ the most modern of techniques—chemotherapy, drug therapy, and advanced psychiatric care.

Finally, a really effective battle against lawlessness must also provide institutions where the general approach of prevention, control and rehabilitation can be planned coherently. I have introduced legislation to create two types: first, a National Institute of Criminal Justice, a new arm of the Executive Branch of the government, which would sponsor broad research and development in the causes of crime and the improvement of every part of the criminal justice process. The results of its work would be disseminated to police departments, courts, prisons, parole and probation officers throughout the country. Second, we should establish in each of the regions in the United States, academies of criminal justice, where students could pursue advanced degrees and enter these fields as professions. These academies would, in addition, provide advanced education for policemen, judges, parole officers, and correction officials. There would be places where the interrelated fields of crime—technology, medicine, law, psychiatry, and social reform—could be discussed by experts. We now have specialized academies for our military, our diplomats, and

[5] Under this pilot program, addicts charged with or convicted of a federal offense can get civil commitment rather than imprisonment if they can benefit from medical treatment. They are placed in medical facilities supervised by the Attorney General and the Surgeon General of the United States. If they respond to treatment they can return to their communities under a carefully supervised program of after-care, which helps them find a job and adjust to life.

our social scientists. These criminal justice academies would hopefully become equally prominent institutions, producing the same caliber of public servants.

Crime cannot be fought with brutal repression, nor with visions of a wholly tranquil community. We will never eliminate all crime and violence. In any society, there will be some citizens, whether motivated by greed or anger, perversity or illness, frustration or ignorance, who cannot live in peace with their neighbors. Our goal must be to limit the damage done by those who choose this path, and to change their direction. In our youth particularly, we must concentrate on extending the chance for community participation to all, eliminating the hopelessness which flourishes when jobs, decent homes, and a stake in the life of the society is lacking. Those whose acts are born out of illness, physical or mental, must be treated. Those who have already broken the law must be reclaimed from a life which injures them, as well as the rest of us. This is not going to be easy; for we first must rouse ourselves from that indifference which is shattered only by the acts of crime, and not by its roots. But unless we focus on both, we shall stand by helplessly while lawlessness flourishes in the 1970s.

THE RACIAL CRISIS

As we look to the next decade, no prospect is more alarming, no trend more dangerous, than the growing distance between black and white America. What began a few years ago as a united, multi-racial, successful challenge to racial injustice has now taken on ominous overtones. Increasingly, black militants are urging separation on their followers, rejecting all cooperation with any part of white society. More dangerously, the spectre of violence has been raised —violence which began with noisy protests, and has led to cities in flames. Men who once urged peaceful change now demand disruption; and the leaders of a youth group whose name pledges nonviolent action preach the violent destruction of the United States.

On April 4, 1968, Americans witnessed a senseless act which took the life of an historic American citizen, the

Reverend Martin Luther King, Jr. His death must be considered part of the pattern of violence that is threatening to take hold of the United States.

This is more than the violence of sick men or racial passion. It is the violence of the individual against society, of group against group. In the last few years we have witnessed many instances of individual and mass violence. Behind the feeling in our hearts that these incidents create, there is the fear that somehow we have lost hold of our communities, that our country is pulling apart into separate peoples who do not know one another: rich and poor, old and young, black and white, where each looks at the other with growing mistrust.

How alien this is to all the hopes and values of America. It is a trend that undermines all our goals, for the finest aspects of material progress will not bring about the nation we want unless the people of this country learn to understand one another and to live together at peace.

The difficult but only road, is for white America to recognize the fundamental injustice of minority life. The difficult but necessary task, is a major and immediate effort to uproot the conditions which keep these men and women from fully participating in the American system. All we lack is the will—the will to see that the greatest threat is not change but our resistance to it.

As the Negro revolution has grown from court tests to peaceful action to calls for "black power," the white community has turned from indifference to sympathy to cold fear. A decade ago, Congress approved an anti-bombing act to curb white violence; the riot control act of 1967 was aimed at blacks. Ten years ago, U.S. troops at Little

Rock were shielding Negroes; in the summer of 1967, units of the New Jersey National Guard rode into riot areas of Newark as white mobs shouted "kill those niggers!" In 1960, both presidential candidates pledged greater efforts to insure equal opportunity. Now a presidential hopeful seeks votes, North and South, on a frank promise to keep the Negro in his place.

It is very possible that this movement could fester until it destroys any hope of cooperation between the races. If white Americans ignore the roots of black discontent, it will spawn even more desperate acts of violence. Those who burn the shops of the ghetto could move to guerrilla raids into the suburbs. The inevitable response to this will be the imposition of curfews in the ghettos, and the restriction of blacks to "their own" neighborhoods. Thus, we will have adopted our own form of South Africa's *apartheid*.

But if we travel this road in the years ahead; if we resign ourselves to guerrilla terror and repressive counter-terror, we shall have succeeded only in ripping apart the fabric of our national life, and destroying permanently our national heritage.

Most white Americans, it appears, do not believe that the racial dilemma is complex. Judging the Negro from their own past, they ask why he remains economically depressed, when every other ethnic group has achieved a secure place in American life? Why have "they" been unable to make progress? Why do so many Negroes appear to flout the pattern of stable family life? And what is it the Negroes want? Haven't they gotten too much already? These are the questions white America must have answered if it is to support the policies needed to prevent the racial crisis from widening.

If white society is now concerned about race, it is from a decidedly narrow spectrum of concern. Charles Silberman, one of the most perceptive writers on this problem, notes that whites "are upset by the current state of race relations, to be sure. But what troubles them is not that justice is being denied, but that their peace is being shattered, and their business interrupted." The Mayor of Newark offered this disturbing observation: "Affluent Americans are gripped more by the need to buy a vacation home, a sports car for their college-bound son, and a second color television set than they are with sharing their affluence with the poor."

This is the attitude which lies behind the backlash, and which spawns the votes for those who hint obliquely about "doing too much for minorities." It is the attitude which is the basis for the belief, probably held by a majority of white Americans, that racial change is occurring too fast. It is an attitude which can be shattered only by a hard, long look at the condition of Negroes in America. It is not a wholly bleak landscape. That progress that has been made, and the effort now continues, is undeniable. But we cannot understand what this progress means unless we understand what remains to be done—and unless we understand how deep are the roots of racial injustice in America.

THE BLACK MAN'S BURDEN

It may seem trivial to note that the Negro came to America as a slave; but it is this experience which sets him apart from any other ethnic group in the United States at the outset. Alone among American strains, the black men came to the land of the free without freedom. My grandfather came to Boston confident he would find liberty, and a chance for a new life. The Negro came to Virginia in chains. For two hundred years, Negroes were, in law and in custom, less than human beings. He was counted three fifths of a man by the United States Constitution, the charter of American liberty. He was deemed a chattel, a thing, by the U. S. Supreme Court, which declared, in the Dred Scott decision, that Negroes "had no rights which the white man was bound to recognize . . . the negro might justly and lawfully be reduced to slavery for [the white man's] benefit." In many Southern states, it was a crime to teach Negroes to read or write.

But slavery meant even more than the denial of liberty; it meant the eradication of cultural stability. Negro families were broken up and sold separately, to bring higher prices. Illegitimacy was encouraged, as a method of "breeding" high priced slaves. What was denied, then, was not only citizenship; it was the essential standards of a civilized being.

This oppression did not end with the 13th amendment. Those who talk blandly about the hundred years the Negro has had to prove himself simply do not know what they are talking about. In the South, the end of slavery was marked by a remarkably swift ascension of Negroes into political and economic power. Under the watchful eye of the federal government, Negroes voted, held office, and traveled freely throughout the mainstream of Southern life. And the white community, despite its resentment, appeared to be resigned to the fact of Negro equality. But after 1876, when federal troops were removed from the South as part of a political compromise surrounding the presidential election of that year, the attitude of the white South changed drastically. Systematically and deliberately white Southern politicians set out to deprive the Negro of the freedoms he was already experiencing.

Thus Mississippi, in revising its state constitution in 1890, declared that "the policy of crushing out the manhood of Negro citizens is to be carried on to success." Carter Glass, a member of Virginia's State Senate and later a prominent national figure, announced that discrimination was the essence of Virginia's constitutional revision of 1901: "that, exactly, is what this convention was elected for —to discriminate to the very extremity of permissible action under the limitations of the Federal Constitution, with a view to the elimination of every Negro voter who can be gotten rid of, legally, without materially impairing the numerical strength of the white electorate." This stratagem worked. In Louisiana, for example, more than 99 percent of the Negro electorate was disenfranchised in the eight years between 1896 and 1904.

Fused with the decline in the need for agricultural labor —the only labor for which the Negro had ever been trained —we can see why the Negro began to flee the South as industrialization began to open up jobs for the unskilled in the North. In the truest sense, the Negro was an immigrant, leaving a land which denied him the stature of a man and the chance to earn his own living. He came North, seeking what all exiles have sought in coming to America: a decent job, a decent home, and a fair chance for a decent life.

The Negro might have expected difficulty in the North.

Every immigrant group, from the Germans in the early nineteenth century, to the Italians and Poles at the end of it, to the Puerto Ricans today, have been greeted with something less than warmth by those who were here before. Many were considered to be "inferior races"—even though they were white. Perhaps the fate of the American Indians, who taught white men how to plant and harvest New World crops, was a powerful lesson in the danger of good will. My own grandfather, searching for employment in Boston, found signs reading No IRISH NEED APPLY. And in New York, immigrants of all cultures and nations banded together in communities within the city, seeking mutual comfort and strength in the midst of a large and hostile new society.

But for the Negro, conditions were different. His past was American—an America of slavery, of rootlessness, of casual, daily inhumanity without even the threads of family life in which to find security and hope. More fundamentally, the strangeness which set him apart from others was incurable; it could not be erased by a generation of public education and a language course. For he had a dark skin; and that was enough to set him apart from his fellows. Other ethnic strains arrived, created political power within Northern communities, and ultimately won acceptance as legitimate autonomous groups. The Negro did not. While others moved ahead, his income stagnated, his neighborhoods became ghettos, and his access to the mainstream of American life continued to remain an empty promise.

This was the nation where all men were created equal; but in the armed forces of America, fighting against racism in World War II, the units of the services were largely

106

segregated, not a single high-ranking officer was a Negro, and most Negroes were relegated to menial servants' tasks; an accurate if brutal reflection of American racial attitudes.

This was the land where anyone with skill and education could gain any job, but at the outset of the Second World War, faced with a critical shortage of skilled mechanics, the president of a major aviation company declared: ". . . It is against company policy to employ [Negroes] as aircraft workers or mechanics . . . regardless of their training. There will be some jobs as janitors for Negroes."

This was the land where the color of a man's skin meant nothing; but in 1955, the schools of our nation's capital were racially segregated; but in 1966, whites and Negroes peacefully marching for open housing were cursed and stoned in Milwaukee and Chicago.

THE BLACK MAN'S ANGER

It would be tempting to assign all this to the realm of the past, and to point to the progress that has been made as the final proof of Negro acceptance. But the facts will not bear this out. If we disregard this 300-year background, and look only at the progress of the Negro, we will find something different than the steady narrowing of the gap between white and black America. The fact is that the Negro is still behind the white man—and he is not only failing to narrow the gap, he is actually further behind than he was before.

At the end of the Second World War, for example, the median family income of whites was about $3150; that of

107

Negro families, little more than $1600. Today, the average white family has an income of more than $6500 a year; while the Negro family has about $3500. The white family, in other words, gained about $3400 in income while the Negro family gained about $1800—and today, despite all the talk of growing equality, the white family is twice as far ahead of his Negro counterpart than he was twenty years ago.

This is one example. The other statistics—in housing, in education, and in comparative achievement based on an equality of skills—all point to the grim fact that for a large percentage of Negroes, the first generation has *not* brought an improvement in status; in fact, it has pushed the Negro further behind the white majority. To put it bluntly, the affluent society is an open, free society—except there is a sign hanging over the door, which reads NOT TOO MANY NEGROES NEED APPLY.

Ironically, this very condition of Negro America has helped to spawn the backlash. We speed by inner-city slums, over expressways on our way to "middle-class" (which means white) suburbs; we hire Negro maids and janitors; we consign black people to their own slums, where they live with a culture, a pattern, and even a language sharply different from our own. We give their schools, their hospitals, their roads, and their people far less than equal treatment. Then we tell ourselves that this is a product of their own flaws; that "they really don't have the energy to do good jobs"; or that "they can't keep their own neighborhoods clean, so it's a good thing we don't let them live near us." We see the Negro—but we do not understand him; and we do not understand that in our own indifference lies the destruction of their lives.

Above all, we do not—because we cannot—understand what it means to be told that effort and talent are useless if a man's skin—your skin—is not the right color. The white man who casually, even amicably, reinforces the belief in Negro inferiority can inflict more pain than the most racist Mississippi Klansman. In his autobiography, the late Malcolm X tells how as an eighth-grade pupil, he consistently won the highest grades in his Midwestern, integrated class, and how he was particularly attached to one teacher. At one point, the teacher asked Malcolm what he wanted to be in life, and Malcolm answered, "a lawyer."

"You've got to be realistic about being a nigger," his teacher replied. "A lawyer—that's no realistic goal for a nigger. You need to think about something you *can* be. You're good with your hands—making things. Why don't you plan on carpentry?"

I wonder, when we look with horror at the growth of open anti-white sentiment in Negro communities, how many of those who preach race hatred learned, as Malcolm X did, to hate in the classroom. How many of them learned with bitterness that the bright pledges of American purpose were not meant for them. And I wonder how we would react if we, or our children, had ever been told that the limits of our lives had been drawn around us by the color of our skins. This, I think, is what James Baldwin must have meant when he wrote that "To be a Negro in this country and to be relatively conscious is to be in a rage almost all the time."

We know now that this rage exists. We know it is being fanned by those who now seek the destruction of American

109

society, out of the delusion that we shall at least all be equal in the rubble of a gutted nation. Without question, we must meet violence with firm and full control. But as we do so, we must realize that until we eliminate the source of this rage, the strong remnants of racial injustice which persist in this nation, we will never curb the spectre of violence, repression and new violence that haunts the coming American decade.

What is needed, put bluntly, is for the majority of Americans to undertake fully the work of providing the Negro, at last, with the chance to be what he can make of himself. It is not a radical or novel principle; indeed, it underlies the very premise of America's belief in individual worth. But it is a principle that we have never permitted the American Negro to exercise.

This response is more than quiescence. To accept the achievements of exceptional black men, to applaud their successes in the world of business, government, sports, or the arts, is not enough. We must rescue those, in our cities, in the rural South, and elsewhere, who have resigned themselves to misery, or who have turned in desperation to acts of solitary or mob violence. This response will require far greater understanding and a massive national effort. But it must be done. "Those who do nothing," President Kennedy said in his civil rights speech of 1963, "are inviting shame as well as violence. Those who act boldly are recognizing right as well as reality."

The most critical areas of this effort lie in these fields:

JOBS

As America learned in the Depression, a community

where those who seek work cannot find it, is a sick community. When men cannot provide for their families, when their days are taken up with aimless, purposeless waiting, their spirit of resignation pervades the community. This is the condition of the Negro world, both North and South. One of every four Negro adults is unemployed; in many urban centers, as many as 50 percent of young people are neither in school nor at work. Yet this is mild comparison with some Black Belt communities of the South. There, where machines have largely replaced Negro unskilled labor, unemployment in some counties is as high as 70 percent.

There are scores of programs on local and state levels to provide those who need jobs with available openings. Recently the federal government, under the Area Redevelopment Act and the Manpower Training Act, has moved into the field. But these programs, broadly speaking, are directed at those with a minimal level of basic education and motivation to take advantage of opportunities. In addition, many State Employment Service organizations are structured as traditional employment agencies, making little effort to reach the hard-core unemployed. While the Job Corps and Neighborhood Youth Corps programs have achieved notable success, the scale of operations is too small, and the difficulties too great, for them to deal with the sweep of joblessness.

The most urgent phase of an employment program is simply to put men to work; to replace welfare rolls with productive, rewarding and promising labor to all who seek it. And the quickest, most effective method of achieving this goal is for the government to become an "employer

111

of last resort"—i.e., to provide jobs to all who need work and cannot find it.

This proposal, which has been advanced by many of our outstanding commentators on the race and poverty problem, and which has recently been suggested by President Johnson, is in no sense a "boondoggle." We need hundreds of thousands more men and women working in the fields of conservation, housing rehabilitation, recreation, hospitals, and schools. Of course this is no ultimate response to unemployment; a hard effort must be made to insure that the first job a man holds will not be his last, and that he will have the chance to develop what talents he has to advance to new employment. But as a matter of urgent national priority, those who seek work must have the chance to work; and if they cannot find it in the private sector, they must be permitted to find it through the government—the same government which pledged, more than twenty years ago, to make full employment a matter of national policy.

But government cannot do the job alone. It must also seek the tools which will help to provide jobs in the private sector to the hard-core unemployed. Here progress is being made. In Los Angeles, an aggressive program of training and recruitment found 6000 jobs for Negroes in Watts. Private firms across the nation are recognizing the need —and the potential—for training the unemployed and the Administration is encouraging them to do so. Government can assist the private sector in a variety of ways, from providing tax incentives to businesses making the effort in job training, to direct subsidization of employment. (Such subsidization might well have other beneficial effects. For

112

example, if supermarkets were to hire the unemployed as clerks, with government providing the difference between the worth of labor and a living wage, customers who now fend for themselves would have the benefit of a return to personal service.)

Similarly, government and private industry could well contract for work-study programs, in which the government pays the cost of training hard-core unemployed, and then provides educational benefits to permit the trainee to learn advanced skills which may lead to promotion.

None of these programs is designed to provide pay without work. Rather, they are aimed at the pathology of hopelessness and resignation which generations of discrimination have bred. If we believe that assertions of fair treatment will erase history, we are kidding ourselves. But if we back up these assertions with large-scale, workable, continuing programs, we may succeed in putting these communities back to work.

HOUSING

The federal government has been involved with housing for almost thirty years; in 1949, Congress declared that every American had a right to decent housing. Today there is more substandard and inadequate housing in our large cities than ever before. Under the urban renewal program, 600,000 low-income housing units have been constructed; but 700,000 units were destroyed in the process. More important, it is now apparent that all too often "urban renewal" meant "Negro removal"—the substitutions of white middle-income areas for Negro neighborhoods.

The shortage of low-income housing—which can be gauged by the existence of more than 5,700,000 substandard housing units in the U.S.—is rooted in hard economic facts. Government must depend on the private construction industry to build low-income housing. But construction costs have risen so fast—more than 20 percent in the last five years alone—that private builders cannot charge rents within the reach of poor families without losing money on their investment. Further, many attempts to provide state subsidization of low-income housing have been rejected by the voters. As a consequence, cities have been forced to stand impotently by as the rising Negro population, fed by high birth rates and continued migration from the South, crowds into housing built decades ago. In New York City, for example, 800,000 people still live in buildings the State legislature back in 1901 declared unfit for human habitation.

To provide adequate housing, substantial changes in existing practices must be made. Many will be unpopular; but the choice is between taking hard decisions now and watching the slow destruction of our urban centers and our domestic tranquillity. These changes are not designed to benefit any minority. They are designed to fulfill a national pledge of decent housing, and to preserve the grandeur of our own major cities.

First, the actual construction costs of new buildings must be lowered. At present, mass production techniques exist which can provide far better low-cost housing than we have now, at far lower cost. Techniques of pre-fabrication and pre-built plumbing and electrical wiring provide potential to construct thousands of new units at the same outlay we are now making.

In order to bring these techniques into operation, however, the labor restrictions in these poverty neighborhoods must be relaxed. They impede the pace and raise the cost of vitally needed low-income housing. This relaxation need not be a threat to overall employment in the building trades industry, as I shall argue later. But with the need for adequate housing approaching the level of a national emergency, those unions which have responded in the past to urgent national needs ought now to recognize that unyielding adherence to outmoded work rules can only impede the development of new patterns of labor, and far greater employment possibilities than now exist.

The first task is to provide an effective, national policy of open housing, in all areas of this nation, city and suburb. On the legal level, this involves a vigorous federal open-housing law. It is a measure of the depth of the racial crisis that enactment of the open-housing bill—the first civil rights act ever to have been aimed at national, rather than regional, racial conditions—was blocked by the Congress. And it is also clear that many white Americans are deeply, passionately afraid of integrated housing; the obscene shouts and the rocks which greeted Negro open-housing marches in Chicago and Milwaukee testifies to that.

This is, in large measure, an economic fear, flowing from the notion that integrated neighborhoods inevitably produce a decline in property values. This is demonstrably untrue. In a comprehensive study of 10,000 transactions involving Negro entry into all-white neighborhoods, six of seven cases resulted in either stable or increased long run property values.

Nonetheless, the fear is there. It has led to invisible color barriers in every city, and elaborate, *sub rosa* real estate practices in which whites are insulated from Negroes —which only breeds more misunderstanding and more fear. And this fear has made possible the despicable practice of "blockbusting," in which real estate dealers panic a neighborhood with tales of a black invasion, buy properties from the fleeing whites at depressed values, sell them to Negroes at a tidy profit, and fulfill their own prophecy by creating all-black neighborhoods.

To change this pattern of housing, it is necessary both to inform and to act. The truth about integrated housing must be brought home to those who fear economic catastrophe if Negroes live next to them. Agencies such as the Community Relations Service can perform a valuable function by actively disseminating this information, particularly in communities where prejudice is more "sophisticated," and more thoroughly disguised under an economic rationale. Both in financial and in human terms, the facts about integration must be made clear. With neighborhoods in Greater Boston, Southeast Washington, and Cleveland now living in racial harmony with stable property values, it is apparent that a better informing job would go a long way in making fair housing a reality.

Beyond information, however, we must take steps which permit Negroes to live where they choose *and* which protect white homeowners against the self-fulfilling prophecy of financial ruin. First we should eradicate the remaining racially restrictive housing practices. The Supreme Court has long forbidden state and local governments from en-

116

couraging in any manner racial discrimination. Soon it may strike down discriminatory practices of major real estate developers. In addition, the Federal Trade Commission has recently outlawed, as a "deceptive trade practice," the policy of advertising housing as open to all when in fact Negroes are barred from occupancy. These acts, fused with vigorous open housing legislation, should put a stop once and for all to denying housing because of race.

These actions, however, must be accompanied by protection for the white homeowner. However untrue the "property values" argument is, it is held as an article of faith by many, perhaps most, white Americans. With the life savings of most families invested in homes, it is easy to understand how fear can be spawned by false facts. The most rational and effective answer to this fear is to guarantee that it will not happen, by insuring the equity in a home.

Similar fears thirty years ago led to runs on banks; the rumor of failure would exhaust a bank's cash supply, and the failure would in fact follow. Once the Federal Deposit Insurance Corporation was founded, however, bank failures dropped sharply. A similar federal insurance to protect the equity invested in a home would be of immeasurable aid in erasing the fear of property loss. (This is not to say that all opposition to "living next to them" would disappear. But it would wipe out the economic argument.)

To further protect the white homeowner, the practice of "blockbusting" through false rumors of Negro invasions should be outlawed. It seems to me apparent that spreading false rumors to drive down property values is as much a fraud, and just as illegal, as the stock and consumer frauds we outlawed long ago. Such legislation would primarily

117

benefit the existing homeowner, insuring that his property is safe from this practice.

These steps would insure the value of private homes. I would suggest further that low-income housing be extended to the suburbs. Here again, suburban communities, reacting with fear to such proposals, have often zoned to outlaw high-density building. In some communities, which have only single family homes on fairly substantial acreages, the reason is to protect the quality of the community. But in other communities, closer to the city, the real reason is to keep Negroes out.

Given the enormous lack of decent inner-city housing, this practice cannot be allowed to continue. In its place, however, we clearly neither want nor should build the high-rise projects which now scar our cities. Instead, suburban communities, architects, and developers should be encouraged to experiment with aesthetically attractive scatter-site low-income housing. Cities like New Haven have already demonstrated attractive and economical alternatives to the high-rise prisons; and most suburbs have nothing to fear from well-planned communities on small scales to provide decent housing for the poor.

HEALTH

America is slowly discovering that its health care is a national disgrace. That the wealthiest nation in the world has an infant mortality rate poorer than sixteen other countries, and that its life expectancy rate is nowhere near as good as far poorer nations, is cause for serious concern. But the harder fact is that it is not "America's" health standards—which are so shocking—it is the health care of

118

the poor, and again, particularly the Negro.

The low-income Negro suffers four times the incidence of heart disease than the national average and ten times the incidence of defective vision. He dies from tuberculosis, flu, and pneumonia—illnesses which medical science cured, for the more affluent of us, long ago. In addition, poor health is a major obstacle to economic achievement. Almost one of three workers who live in poverty areas suffer from physical disabilities which affect job performance. A recent national survey of welfare recipients shows physical ailments a major cause of unemployment among the poor.

In most communities, the poor are served through charitable hospitals and clinics. But this system of health care has in fact reinforced the ill health of the poor. Medical care for the ghetto is not medical care in the sense that we think of it. The personal relationship with a doctor, which is supposed to form the basis of our medical system, does not exist. Instead, there is a confusing web of clinics, outpatient rooms, emergency room corridors filled with overburdened and necessarily uninterested staffs, and long lines of people waiting for cursory treatment. The effect of this structure on medical care is clear: in some ghetto areas, as many as 30 percent of the people have never had a checkup. And fewer than half of the expectant mothers ever see a doctor during the critical early months of pregnancy.

A vital change in this pattern is to bring medical services closer to the ghetto communities, away from the distant and remote giant clinics and hospitals. One such method, which I proposed as an amendment to the war on poverty program and which is now in operation, establishes neighborhood health centers within the framework of the Community Action programs. These neighborhood centers use store fronts and space in housing projects, and are staffed by both well-trained personnel and by community representatives, trained for routine medical duties.

Only thirty-five of these centers have been funded. But the work they have done demonstrates this kind of approach holds great promise. If we expanded this program to provide at least one health center for every 25,000 inhabitants, we would be on our way toward bringing medical care to those who need it most. And given the response of hospitals such as New York's Albert Einstein College of Medicine, I am convinced that we would find in the medical schools a group of committed and concerned medical students, eager to emulate the law school students who work in Neighborhood Legal Assistance.

As we make the medical system more flexible, I believe we must also attract far more Negroes into the health professions at all levels. The need for trained nurses, medical aides, and doctors can be met, at least in part, by a program of active recruitment and financial assistance. I thus proposed last year a series of new programs to encourage ghetto residents to enter the health profession, through scholarships, stipends, and research and demonstration projects. We have already seen, through programs like those of the Student Health Organizations in Chicago and Los Angeles, that medical, dental and nursing students can be used in ghetto areas both to learn and to bring medical care to those in need. Similarly, those we train could go back into their neighborhoods with the badly needed skills they have learned.

EDUCATION

The evidence is in on the job our educational system has done for the Negro; and the verdict is not a happy one. Education, which for millions of new and poor Americans has been the key to success, has become for the Negro a dreary institution which confirms his place as a second-class citizen.

I would suspect that most Americans believe education has produced a steady improvement in the achievement of ghetto children. The fact is that the process of education appears to stifle the ability of the children, and to render them unfit for participation in society. Startling as it sounds, the reading level and IQ scores of children in New York's ghetto schools *drops* between the third and sixth grade; and now, after thirty years of effort, the achievement gap between white and Negro youngsters in that city is wider than it was thirty years ago. One young writer who taught in a Boston ghetto school—and who was dismissed after reading his children a poem written by a Negro author—has bitterly described the fruits of education in the title of his book: *Death at an Early Age*.

The secret of what to do about ghetto education is no secret at all; the answer is to *change what we have been doing and change now*. It is astonishing that professionals, whether writers, teachers, or administrators, should point to the failure of children as evidence of the child's inferiority. What it proves is that the schools, by retaining processes which have not worked for decades, are failing

121

in their job. Using textbooks, methods, and strategies to which children will not respond is as senseless as teaching them in a foreign language.

The steps which must be taken are many. We can begin by taking the lessons of the Headstart program into the classroom, using community people, mothers of pre-school children, and high school students as teachers for the earlier grade children. Teaching by rote can be scrapped in favor of innovative techniques which talk about the world the ghetto child knows—not the world of Dick and Jane and farms and suburbs. New texts and substitutes for textbooks have already been marketed. They should be employed as soon as possible.

Further, schools within the ghetto should be staffed as would a hospital in a disaster area; for this is exactly what the ghetto school is. The best educators on campuses should be brought into the schools, to work with (not on) the community as advisors and implementers. And the shamefully inadequate physical facilities must be brought up-to-date. Title II of the Elementary and Secondary Education Act has been of some help; but the funds must be concentrated more to meet the needs of the poorest of schools, both in the city and in our rural communities.

Fundamentally, however, it is the structures of education which must be altered. I have already discussed in Chapter I how communities within large cities could gain a greater role in the administration of the schools. In addition to this change, the size of schools might well be reduced, to return to a close-knit community instead of the oversized castles in which ghetto children now learn how not to learn. The stringent requirements for those seeking teaching degrees must be replaced by a more flexible set of criteria, which focus on what prospective teachers and administrators can do for the children. When a man like New York's Elliot Shapiro, who has won the love of the children and the community in his ghetto school, can be opposed for promotion because he failed to take the proper courses, we know a change in attitude is necessary. Those who demand rigid professional criteria might well look about them and see what these standards have produced. There is little danger in change, for the hard fact is that ghetto schools can hardly become less effective than they are now.

I would hope that with improvements in ghetto education, sparked by increased federal funding, will come greater use of pupil exchanges with white areas. The communities around Boston have experimented with some success in opening undercrowded suburban schools to children from the inner-city. It has broadened the sights of both the white and the Negro children and assisted understanding in both white and black communities. Those suburbs whose people have enough concern and maturity not to shut themselves off from the city may well find that their own children benefit as much as the visiting children from this important experiment in learning and democracy.

Education, however, cannot stop at the public school level. Higher education has become a necessity for full participation in the economic life of America. Yet today almost all Negroes are effectively banned from college by economic hardship. Despite the welcome increase in scholarship programs, only 30 percent of Negro high school graduates go on to college, and many of these go to all-

Negro southern colleges, where education is not an adequate preparation for integrated lives.

The most helpful answer here is a greatly accelerated program of federal scholarships and long-term, low-interest loans. I believe that at least 75,000 scholarships a year ought to be provided immediately by such a program. For every generation of Negro children denied a college education is a generation whose skill, talent and ability has been lost to our nation, and who have been denied the American promise of reaching the limits of their ability.

To those who ask where the funds come from, I think the answer is clear. Existing methods of financing education, largely linked to the real estate property tax, has proven obsolete. As a matter of plain fact, these taxes cannot be raised much higher in our large cities without crippling them. Instead, the federal government, whose funds come from the graduated income tax, will inevitably be assuming more of the burden. Title I of the Elementary and Secondary Education Act of 1965 is an explicit recognition that the federal government must help communities meet the special educational needs caused by large numbers of low-income families. This has been a good program; it must be expanded, and concentrated to meet the hardest hit of our educational areas.

COMMUNITY POWER

As I have discussed in Chapter I, it is essential that communities within our largest metropolitan areas be given financial and political power to shape their own neigh-

124

borhoods, and the lives they lead. This has particular importance to the Negro, long assumed to be either unwilling or unable to build his own structures. Today, black communities are shattering this myth, to the dismay of many white onlookers. They are creating their own banks, credit companies, and business organizations to prevent outside control of community sources of wealth. They are demanding that programs to improve their lot be run by those whose lives are to be changed. They are seeking the power they were so long assumed not to want.

To accept this trend and to work with it is the most promising path for the white community to take. I believe last fall's elections in Gary, Indiana, and Cleveland, Ohio, showed that white voters will accept the election of able and responsible Negroes to high office and some will even support them.

This is a healthy trend, and should be encouraged, rather than feared. Just as every ethnic group has created its own institutions—social, economic, political—so the Negro is at last recognizing his own capabilities. It was distressing that the Congress voted to deprive these communities of effective control of poverty projects; for this act only reinforced the sense of outside control which can spawn hostility. But we dare not compound this error by misreading the growth of community power.

THE SOUTHERN NEGRO

In the last few years, the nation's attention has turned to our cities. But there are still 6,000,000 Negroes in the

125

rural and small town South, leading quieter but even more depressing lives than their Northern counterparts (we can gauge the comparative desirability by noting that a recent estimate predicted millions of these will move into large cities from the rural areas in the coming decade). The civil rights movement, born in the South, has moderated legal discrimination. But fewer than 15 percent of Southern Negroes attend integrated schools; the right to vote still has not brought anything like full participation in society; and the economic growth of the South has largely bypassed the Negro.

Rural Negroes in the South do not riot. They move North, unprepared for urban problems and unskilled for available employment. And they find, too often, only hopelessness and frustration.

The proper approach, I think, is to provide greater opportunity within the rural South. Agriculture is still a worthwhile and productive possibility, if modern methods can be used. If we encourage the replacement of sharecropping with cooperatively owned farms, through the use of long-term government loans, we might see a surprising growth in Negro agricultural productivity.

Given government assistance in crop diversification and production, these cooperatives—as experiments in Alabama and Georgia have shown—may hold the promise for a just Negro participation in the Southern communities. We know what county agent programs have done in the past for farmers; now the government can both help rural areas improve the economic life of rural Negroes and prevent even greater pressure on the overcrowded cities.

THE "WHITE" PROBLEM

All these programs will take effort and money. But they are far from a threat to whites. In almost every sense, the commitment to eliminate racial injustice will produce tangible benefits to the white majority, as well as honoring our heritage.

For example: welfare costs now burden the working tax-payer more each year. At present, the government spends almost $5 billion each year on public assistance—and this figure does not include state and local expenditures. A program in which men were put to work would replace welfare recipients with tax-paying citizens, lowering the relief rolls and broadening the tax base. Providing low-income housing would be a great benefit to established workers. As projects expand, so would the need for supervisory training, and so would the opportunities for promotion among those already skilled. As educational ability increased, so would the supply of teachers and skilled workers to meet the rapidly growing job needs of America in the next decade. And ultimately, as economist Barbara Ward noted, the equal status of Negroes could mean as much as $23,-000,000,000 yearly in national productivity—a gain which would be reflected in the status of each of us.

The "white" problem, then, is for us, as the relatively comfortable and affluent majority, to recognize that a grave wrong has been done to a minority; and that we are threatened not by change, but by continued indifference to it. It is time, at long last, to recognize the essential, un-

127

deniable, still-ignored truth that racial discrimination is no part of a civilized society.

It is also a problem of will; but that is a problem which cannot stand in the way of change. We spend today $3,000,000,000 every month to defend the freedom of 14,000,000 people in South Vietnam. We could certainly afford to make a far greater effort than we have for the freedom and the future of 22,000,000 black people, here in America, whose freedom and future is intertwined with ours. No foreign commitment, in Vietnam or anywhere else, is so great that it can excuse continued acceptance of racial injustice.

The task of change will not be one for any one administration; it is the work of a generation. I would like to think it can and will be accomplished by this younger generation, white and black, which first stirred the national conscience. This is not a certain prophecy. There were youths who taught Negro children in Mississippi, and youths who hurled stones at Negroes in Chicago. And there are many more who will be content to remain in their affluence, blind to the sufferings of other human beings and to the storm that such suffering is breeding.

But there is still the chance for change, still the hope that these young people who do care, and who have acted, will turn the concern of their youth into the concern of a lifetime. If they can challenge the rest of America with simple moral courage and complex practical effort, we can avoid going the route of a racist nation, apart and afraid. And we can become, to that extent, the generation of Americans which at last redeemed the promise of equality and human dignity.

128

PART II

ABROAD

EUROPE: THE PARADOX OF SUCCESS

In the field of foreign policy, our primary aims during the 1970s should be to try to end the cold war that has dominated world politics for the past twenty years, and to help bring about economic progress in the poor nations. Based on the changes that have taken place in recent years, and the forces in motion in the world, I think there is a good chance to accomplish these ends without endangering our own national interests. But we can only do it if we begin to put aside outmoded policies, and adopt new ones which, without sacrificing security, lessen tensions and moderate differences between nations.

In no part of the world have events outrun our policies faster than in the continent of Europe. After the Second World War, Europe's industrial and economic might lay scattered in rubble. Soviet troops occupied all of Eastern

131

Europe; and this force, added to internal instability, threatened the political survival of France, Italy, Greece, Turkey, and Austria. Our policies in Europe—political, military, and economic—were directed of necessity to the Communist threat.

Western Europe today is a prosperous society, with growth rates far outstripping our own. The moribund economies which faced the Marshall Plan have been replaced by healthy, vibrant industrial machines. Eastern Europe too, has grown economically; and that growth has increased her desire to trade with her neighbors to the west. Such trade now exceeds $8,000,000,000 a year; and this trade has, in turn, led to growing contacts between the two regions. What used to be the Iron Curtain separating East and West Europe has become a grillwork, through which the natural ties between industrial states are being formed.

Equally as dramatic has been the change of Russia's position in Europe. Twenty years ago, the Soviet Union commanded a string of satellite states, totally submissive to her economic and political wishes. Today, with the exception of East Germany, Russia has no more satellites. Most of the Communist nations of Europe are, of course, ideologically allied with the Soviet Union. Russian troops are still on their soil, and trade remains primarily with Russia. But consider what has changed since the 1940s: Rumania has all but declared her independence, as did Yugoslavia and Albania years ago. She has opened new relations with West Germany, kept relations with the Chinese, failed to participate in Warsaw bloc maneuvers, and refused to follow her Communist neighbors in support of the Arab position in the Mideast. Czechoslovakia has proposed

132

Eastern European military arrangements that exclude Russia. Poland and Hungary permit surprising degrees of intellectual criticism of the Soviet Union; and throughout Eastern Europe, youth openly treat Russia as a bureaucratic nation which cannot command their allegiance. Russian leaders rush to Eastern European capitols, seeking to coordinate policies on issues (like East Germany) she used to be able to order by fiat. The Czech Communist Party recently ousted its leader, despite a personal plea from Leonid Brezhnev. Even to keep her troops in Eastern Europe, Russia has been forced to negotiate status-of-forces agreements, similar to our own. Where she used to treat these nations as colonies, Russia now sends raw material to Hungary and Czechoslovakia to supply their growing industries.

The change that has swept across Europe has not left the United States alone. Western Europe is no longer a weak and threatened area, dependent on American economic aid and military protection, willingly subordinating its policies to ours. These countries, with centuries of nationalist tradition, are finding that they have the strength to reassert their own identities. In this sense, "Gaullism" is not the aberrational belief of one man, nor confined to one nation. A thrust for national independence will be the dominant feature of Europe for some time to come. (This should not surprise us, nor should it be explained with the accusation of "ingratitude." Less than twenty years after France gave the United States crucial assistance in winning her independence, we remained studiously neutral in her own difficulties, and engaged in a series of bitter diplomatic disputes that almost resulted in war.)

133

Europe is not at the center of our concern today. When American lives are at stake in a small Asian nation, this is where the focus of our attention will be. Yet it is worth remembering that for a decade and a half, Europe was the crucible of American foreign policy. It was the only place on earth where American armies faced Russian armies across a border, at times perilously close to action. As recently as 1961, United States National Guard and Reserve forces were mobilized—not because of Vietnam, but because of tensions over Berlin.

As the crisis atmosphere disappears from Europe, so may our interest. It is easier, in foreign policy, to react to obvious dangers than to seize new opportunities. But it is senseless to posit a policy on threats which do not exist, and which the nations we deal with do not feel. And it is wasteful not to recognize the promise that the future holds in Europe. It appears that the chance has finally arrived for the achievement of lasting, even permanent peace and stability in Europe. And this achievement would threaten no one. Every European nation, democratic or Communist, knows that peace and stability would be in its own interest. Each of them is more concerned with developing economically than with exporting revolution. This is too hopeful a promise to be dissipated, either by our own apathy or by stubborn adherence to obsolete policies.

Our ultimate hopes for Europe need to be clear. As I see it, what we hope for is a continent, from the Irish Sea to the borders of Asia, which has relations free of tensions and restrictions; a Europe in which unification will develop politically, as it has economically and technologically. It would be a Europe where the lingering fears of World

War II are dissipated; one where Germany, assured of her own security, can reunite without being considered a threat to the security of others; one where the military structures of the Cold War were clearly no longer needed, and where the Warsaw Pact, NATO, and the presence of foreign troops could be eliminated, as the needs which created them disappear. It would be a Europe of nations providing for their own security, jointly or separately, supported by American and Soviet nuclear guarantees.

The goal, in short, is to achieve a *détente* between ourselves, and Russia in which European countries could freely join. This, the final end of the Cold War in Europe, should be the goal of our policies on that Continent in the 1970s.

But these goals are hopes, not a policy. It is imperative that we understand the distinction; for if we justify irrational or harmful policies by pointing to the nobility of our goals, we only delude ourselves, and may in fact harm the ultimate realization of a Europe fully at peace. Our own efforts must be far more modest, far more realistic, and always based on the understanding that it is Europe which will determine her own destiny.

TOWARD EUROPEAN UNIFICATION

We believe, for example, that European unification is an important continental policy. It was an objective of the Marshall Plan; it was a specific aim even in the NATO Charter; we were strongly behind a Common Market as early as 1949, and supported an all-European army in the early 1950s. In part, this reflects our own fondness for federalism. In part, it reflects the philosophy of some of the best of Europe's statesmen, such as Jean Monnet, the "father" of the Common Market. We support unification even though it is not in our own economic interest, because it is an element of a peaceful and stable Europe.

But it is not at all clear that vigorous American support for unification has helped achieve this goal. Our efforts to influence admission to the Common Market and the acceptance of multi-lateral defense ties may have harmed unification, rather than helped it. It may well be that an America which finds itself leading, rather than assisting, such unification may be raising suspicions about whose interests unification helps.

We have already seen that the most disruptive strains of European nationalism are focusing on what they claim are American attempts to assert continuing dominance over Europe; that the threat of "the American challenge"—in clothes, language, culture, and economy—is taken seriously by many Europeans. If integration is assumed to be a United States-based goal, then it will not be willingly accepted. Further, a preoccupation with unification may impede other long-range goals. Russia, for example, will not loosen its continuing grip on the East if it appears to her that the United States is attempting to maintain dominance in Western Europe.

We should, in short, understand that nationalism in Europe is no less prevalent than in the underdeveloped world, or indeed here in the United States. Economic integration, exchange of workers and skills, the lowering of trade barriers: these trends will accelerate as the natural impetus of industrialization takes hold. But let us not set back this trend by excessive intercession on behalf of it. As President Kennedy said in Frankfurt in 1963, "The choice of paths to the unity of Europe is a choice Europe must make." The nations of Europe should work out the further steps toward integration on their own, assured of our help if they ask for it, but secure in the knowledge that we do not wish to dominate the arrangements they make.

As we recognize that the pace of unification may not please us, we should also anticipate the problems which it may bring. An industrialized Europe is, after all, a natural competitor of other industrialized nations, including ours. Her exports to the United States have increased by 400 percent in the last fifteen years; and European direct investment in America has tripled since 1950, to more than $6,000,000,000. This economic health was a prime goal of our postwar policy; it is a "threat" to be met by vigorous competition, not by repressive trade measures. We should understand that Europe will be jealous of maintaining her economic strength. Her talent and her resources are not ours for the asking. We should not skim off her best brains for our industries. We must respond with prudence and care to European economic policies aimed at us, in the hope that healthy trading patterns can be achieved. And let us remember, too, that economic policy differences will be a small price to pay for a strong Europe, working with us in the overriding task of assisting the underdeveloped world.

NATO

Another key area of reassessment is military policy; particularly the nature and size of our troop commitment, and the role of NATO. NATO's original assignment was to meet the military danger of Stalinist Russia. Born at a time of international tension, war in Korea, and the reality of two hundred Russian divisions in Eastern Europe, NATO has proven an effective deterrent. Its original strategic purpose was to hold off the numerically superior Communist forces from overrunning Europe to the English Channel, until American atomic air power could be brought into play against Russian cities. It gave the Soviets a very real risk to balance before starting an invasion. It has helped keep the peace for over fifteen years.

It is highly questionable, however, that NATO as now organized is meaningful. It is aimed, let us remember, at a threat which almost no one in Europe considers likely any longer. Even those who feel Russia might still start a war under appropriate circumstances agree that the real deterrent to such a move, and the most effective way of combatting it, is through American nuclear weapons, which we hold independent of NATO. And those who look at the possibility of a push against Berlin find it hard to believe that, in itself, would provoke nuclear response by America. The removal of French troops from NATO may have been in part political; but it was also a clear sign that France simply did not consider NATO essential to its own defense. And we have seen that efforts to avoid nuclear proliferation through NATO have not been successful. The abortive Multi-Lateral Force, contemplating joint participation in nuclear-armed weapons systems, raised strong fears of German nuclear control; and such fears, it is apparent, will continue into the next decade.

All this suggests that at present NATO is better suited to yesterday's dangers than to tomorrow's opportunities. We must begin asking some difficult questions about this institution. Do we believe, for example, that the Soviet Union is still interested in a military attack on Western Europe? Could such an attack, if ever planned, come in a way that could be met by NATO? Have we encouraged European dependency on U.S. forces, in effect making NATO an American force? Are we perpetuating this dependency by forcing European nations to buy American weapons, thus discouraging them from developing independent defenses? And does it help the interests of NATO nations to concentrate so much NATO planning in the Pentagon, rather than in the European capitals?

To these questions must be added an inquiry about the size of U.S. troop strength in NATO. General Eisenhower, for example, has suggested we could fulfill our commitments to NATO with two divisions instead of the five divisions and two brigades we now have, totalling 235,000 men. Senator Mike Mansfield has urged similar reductions be made. This possibility, I believe, opens the way to a reduction of forces in both Eastern and Western Europe. Through a joint agreement with the Soviet Union, we could agree to withdraw these four divisions as Russia withdrew a proportionate number. Alternatively, we might attempt a dual-basing system, leaving equipment in Europe and re-

139

turning our troops to the United States. In this manner, we might assure our allies that these troops would be available if needed, while contributing to a reduction in European military tension.

NATO does not appear to be susceptible to revival through political roles. Some have advocated a NATO which coordinates Western moves toward *détente* with the East, or which speaks for the Atlantic community in matters other than European. This is not harmful, unless the U.S. pushes this policy without European support. But it does not appear that the European nations would cede meaningful political power to NATO.

The need for change, however, does not mean that the structure of NATO should be dissolved. NATO is still the only existing military defense in Western Europe. It should not end until Europe perfects an adequate defense system of its own. We should, rather, coordinate NATO policy with our clear-cut policy of reducing to a minimum our military strength in Europe, and replacing present structures with forces solely European. We should remember that NATO is not an icon; its purpose at the outset was explicitly temporary. As one famous American general said in 1950, "We don't expect this to be here five years from now." Once the military future of Europe is settled, we can and should retire NATO as a valuable tool which has fulfilled its purpose.

The next decade, then, should begin the reduction of American involvement in the military and economic affairs of Europe. But this is in no sense a call to isolation. It would be a grave mistake to turn our backs on Europe, or forget her when crisis in Asia or the Middle East turns our

140

attention elsewhere. Where to press and where to relax is the essence of leadership in foreign policy. There are initiatives we can take which can help Europe achieve the hopes we have for it.

HOPES FOR NON-PROLIFERATION

For example, we should exert our leadership to get agreements designed to lessen tensions and the possibility of war, such as the non-proliferation treaty. In a treaty of this nature, nations that have nuclear weapons promise not to introduce them into countries that do not; and nonnuclear powers promise not to receive or develop them. A non-proliferation agreement is valuable for its own sake, representing as it does the most significant step toward arms control that we and the Soviets have so far taken together. But it would have additional benefits for stability in Europe. It would greatly reduce the fear of a revived, militaristic and nuclear-powered Germany—an unjustified fear in my judgment, but one which is still used to erect barriers to the normalization of Europe. Even if the final treaty exempts a future European nuclear force, the fear of Germany would have no basis. The force would be composed of British and French weapons with mutual assistance and a share of control by Germany and the other nations. Thus, any German use of these weapons would be checked and controlled by some of her former enemies. And even if non-nuclear nations were allowed to develop nuclear energy, including earth-moving explosives, for peaceful uses, under inspection, the vital part of non-proliferation

141

—the control of arms—would remain. In fact, American and Russian technicians could even be made available to the non-nuclear countries in their development of peaceful uses, so that they would not be put at a technological disadvantage if, in the future, nuclear technology becomes important to economic progress.

The non-proliferation treaty recently signed by the United States and Russia has met with criticism by non-nuclear countries, which feel we are asking them to disarm while we maintain our own nuclear strength. To achieve it, we may have to find a way to guarantee these nations against nuclear attack or nuclear blackmail by their adversaries. I hope such a treaty, taken with the Nuclear Test Ban Treaty of 1963, can be just the first two steps in a pattern of planned and safe disarmament. Further steps should include reducing American and Russian reliance on nuclear weapons in our own defense establishments.

GERMANY AND BERLIN

We should further support efforts to take the danger of war out of the East-West conflict in the middle of Germany. This is still the primary danger point in Europe, one of the few places where relations remain at Cold War temperatures. While the goal of our policy should be the reunification of Germany, we should realize that before this must come an evolutionary process. It must begin with greater contacts between the two parts of Germany. It will grow as they recognize the mutual benefit from closer relations in trade, traffic, and cultural relations. Reunification of Germany is necessarily the last in a long line of relaxations and mutual accommodations on the continent of Europe. As a practical matter, it must await the withdrawal of foreign troops from Germany. This withdrawal cannot come until the East-West confrontation in Germany, with its perpetual danger of armed conflict, disappears. But that confrontation can best be moderated if the two parts of Germany begin to talk and work with each other.

West Germany, we know, finds itself in a difficult situation in its attempts to insure its own security while looking toward a peaceful European settlement. Its approaches to East Germany have so far been rebuffed. Part of the reason could be West Germany's refusal to deal with East Germany as a *de facto* entity. East Germany, certainly the most insecure nation in the world, sees West German diplomatic overtures to her Eastern neighbors as a plot to isolate it. West Germany is surrounded by sensitive nations with long memories. She deserves our support in the important new initiatives she has proposed to ease tension in the middle of Europe, and in her feeling that better relations with the East, far from implying acceptance of Germany's division, brings eventual reunification closer.

There are distinguished experts on Eastern Europe who feel that if the West freezes out East Germany, the country's old-line Stalinist policies will be so embarrassing to the rest of Eastern Europe that they will eventually seek to abolish it as a separate entity. I do not think this is necessary. East Germany has grown more prosperous in recent years. We can take the calculated risk that she will throw off some of the fixtures of Communism as she rises economically, as her Communist neighbors have already done.

We have nothing to fear from an East Germany which finds it can improve itself through more ties with the West. The history of the other former satellite countries shows that this is the way to relaxation. And it is certainly the best route to the vital goal of reunification of Germany.

In the meantime, we must react carefully to any disturbance that might grow out of the confrontation in Germany. At the present writing, there is a strong possibility that East Germany, in retaliation for the diplomatic initiatives of the Grand Coalition, might try to precipitate another Berlin crisis. One closed checkpoint, one stopped convoy, one plane strayed across a border, could cause an incident, which could trigger a crisis, which, in turn, could wash away all the progress that has been made toward normalization over the past seven years.

We cannot tell when this might happen, nor can we prevent it. If in fact an incident represents a real threat to the security of West Berlin, we would have to respond to it as such, and we should keep a military capacity there which can do so. But the Soviets do not seem to be as interested in challenging the West in Berlin as they were in Khrushchev's time. For all their blustering statements, they seem to be trying both to placate and restrain the cold warriors of East Germany. In making our response we should be careful to separate East German interests from Russian interests. This could help us to distinguish between a mere incident, and a serious challenge to our legal rights and West Berlin's freedom.

We are in a much more fluid situation in relation to the nations of the Communist world. We can have a direct confrontation in Vietnam and take steps to counter the

144

disturbing expansion of Soviet influence in the Middle East, but at the same time we can establish consular relations and work together on such important security issues as nuclear proliferation. We did not let Syngman Rhee sabotage the truce in Korea by letting the prisoners of war escape. Nor should the Soviet Union allow a desperate East German government to trigger a new Berlin crisis which could drag Europe back to the 1950s.

EASTERN EUROPE

In addition, we should continue to build bridges in Eastern Europe, of the kind President Johnson spoke of in his historic address in October 1965, and of the kind advocated by Republican Senators Thruston B. Morton and Charles H. Percy. These policies, in addition to reducing international tensions, appear to have helped the peoples of these nations as well; for the liberation of East Europe from the most repressive features of Communist life has come not by armed intervention or internal revolution, but by the gradual vitalization of the levers of freedom within these nations. As foreign trade grows, so does greater understanding. The shackles of bureaucratic rigidity loosen as governments realize that they simply do not aid industry and commerce. Thus, in Yugoslavia, movement is underway to remove Communist Party cells from policymaking functions within plants and factories.

We welcome the kind of improvement that has taken place in relations between West Germany and the countries of Rumania and Czechoslovakia. But I would hope that the

145

barriers might begin to fall, as well, in the much more difficult impasse between West Germany and Poland. The position taken by the Catholic bishops of Poland, favoring such contacts, was courageous and enlightened on their part, and could signal a beginning.

To encourage these trends, the widest possible contacts between the two Europes—and between Eastern Europe and the United States—should be encouraged. For example, East European nations might be encouraged to participate in the Organization for European Cooperation and Planning. International funds, backed with capital from the Soviet Union and the United States, could encourage joint economic and industrial projects. And, in an effort to increase trade contacts, our own nation could adjust its policies. We accomplish nothing, for example, by denying most favored nation status in our tariff policy to Eastern European nations, except the continued breeding of mistrust and injury to our own businessmen. Similarly, no one was aided by the cutoff of American assistance to Italy in building a Fiat plant in the Soviet Union. These shortsighted policies work only to maintain military and political hostility within Europe. That is in no one's interest, least of all our own.

All these steps can be taken cautiously. But the bridges we build to promote healthy national independence will eventually cause political changes in Communist nations. And there is no doubt that treating these nations *as if* they are independent of the Soviet Union helps them to *become* so.

In the early days of our country, the major goal of American foreign policy was to stay out of Europe's internal affairs. A hundred and fifty years, and two wars fought for her freedom and ours, have now brought us full cycle, to a point where less involvement and direction by us, and more support of European initiatives, would serve the needs of both of our continents. Of all the foreign continents, Europe will probably always be closest to our lives. We have a common history, culture, and political system. She should be in the center of our policy concern —not in the backwash. But if that concern counsels restraint on our part, we should exercise it.

The ending of the cold war in Europe will not solve all her problems. It will not insure representative regimes in Eastern Europe, or democracy in Russia, or an end of the fear of Germany, or of any of the difficulties created by the deep scars of history and the independent course of proud and nationalistic states. But it will bring to an end the conditions that brought our troops to Europe in the first place. It will lessen the number of enemies we have in the world. It will allow us to concentrate more resources in parts of the globe that desperately need our aid. And most important, it will allow Europe to turn some of its resources to the help of the less developed nations of the world. For this is where the real test is going to come in the next generation, and neither the United States nor Europe are giving them the help that they must.

147

ASIA: THE PERILS OF
OVERCOMMITMENT

Today our attention is focused on Asia; but it is a focus scarred by the horror of a war we did not seek and do not want. Whatever the wisdom of this costly war, few would deny that we fight now not only because of commitment, but because of errors of judgment made repeatedly about the realities of Vietnam.

At this writing the war in Vietnam has entered another year of bloodshed and grim American involvement. The courage of our soldiers is undeniable. But at home there is a growing realization that our obligation to the people of Vietnam now call for less war, not more, and negotiations soon rather than later.

The kind of war we are fighting in Vietnam will not gain the long range objectives we have there. The widespread destruction we are creating will only make a workable political future for that country more difficult. Moreover, the government we are supporting in Vietnam does not have its heart in the cause of the people and offers no indication that it can win their lasting confidence.

If negotiations are not forthcoming there, or if they face a great delay, we should begin to moderate significantly our military activities to levels more commensurate with the limited aims we have there. We should adopt a more military posture designed to protect and hold areas of heavy population in order to maximize the safety and security of the Vietnamese people rather than to search out and destroy the enemy.

For too long we have tolerated corruption and indifference among the rulers of Saigon. We have not confronted them with the same determined fury we have unleashed on Hanoi. We must settle with them the entire question of their corruption, inefficiency and the waste of American resources and the future of the pacification program. We should make it clear that we cannot continue year after year picking up the pieces of their own failures. We should do all that is necessary to help the Saigon government prepare to take over its responsibilities, but if they are unwilling to do so, they should know that the American people, with great justification, could well consider our responsibilities fulfilled.

By the 1970s, hopefully, the war in Vietnam will have ended, as far as American participation is concerned. Our task then will be to avoid the errors of judgment that have mired us so deeply in that small and tragic nation.

Thus, even if we are not clear about what we want in Asia, the record is brutally clear about what we do not

149

want. We want no more bloody, divisive battles which turn us away from peace abroad and progress at home, dividing our own nation and darkening our relations with others. Vietnam is not the only small nation in Asia that is moving through a period of tension. Unless we clearly understand the goals that we are pursuing in Asia, and unless we have the understanding to pursue those goals with prudent methods, we may find ourselves—as we have three times in the last eighteen years—fighting with American troops on the Asian mainland. The central task of an Asian policy for the 1970s, then, is in a sense negative. It is to avoid those errors of judgment and understanding which led us to war in Vietnam. But it should also be positive; to construct a basis for peaceful relations with peoples of the Pacific and the Asian continent.

It is easy to express our hopes for Asia. We hope to see the peoples of Asia living in peace, developing their own nations for their own people, free from coercion, or terror, or aggression, free to follow their own cultural and religious traditions. Our goal in Asia as elsewhere is, as President Kennedy said, "to make the world safe for diversity."

It would be a fatal mistake, however, to assume that our political and social aspirations—indeed, even our frame of reference—can be superimposed on the Asian peoples. The Asian societies, diverse, complex, and far more venerable than those of the West, rise out of distinct cultures and experiences, which are not ours. We can and should help these societies to preserve their autonomy in the face of clear-cut aggression. But we cannot react to Asian developments as we would if the same events took place here, or in Europe.

150

This was, in large measure, just what we did *not* understand when we became politically entwined with Asia after the Second World War. We came fresh from successes with a massive European recovery plan, and an original attempt to fuse Western Europe into a military shield against Soviet expansion. We applied many of the same assumptions that were correct in Europe to wholly different Asian conditions. With the collapse of Chiang Kai-shek's government in China, which we analogized closely to the Communist takeover of Eastern Europe, we assumed the applicability of our European experience.

The implementation of our European assumptions, complete with illusory military alliances and inapplicable "development" programs has brought us today to our uneasy Asian position. We are probably more deeply enmeshed in Asia than anywhere else in the world, including areas where our national interests are far more direct and immediate. Besides the obvious case of Vietnam, we support one of the factions in Laos; we pay the armies of Thailand, Taiwan, and to a large extent South Korea; we protect Taiwan and the Pescadores Islands from Red Chinese invasion; we stand guard on the 38th Parallel of Korea; our immense Seventh Fleet controls the coastal waters of East Asia. We support these operations with more than sixty military bases in the Pacific Ocean area. More than five thousand people work out of our Asian embassies, in addition to an undisclosed number of intelligence personnel, and 280,000 troops are stationed there, outside of Vietnam. What we have built, then, is a massive official American presence in Asia. The most difficult, yet most urgent question for us to determine in the next decade is whether this

151

power is justifiable: whether the peace and progress we seek can best be achieved by a maintenance or a reduction in our Asian involvement.

I think it is clear that this presence has at times harmed, rather than promoted, our national interests. Unlike Western Europe, whose nations were composed of established, functioning Western institutions, many of the Asian nations lacked strong political tradition in anything like a Western sense. In these nations, searching for stability, we identified ourselves far too closely with specific regimes, until their perpetuation became, by inadvertence, an American commitment. Many of these regimes—Syngman Rhee in Korea, General Phoumi Nosavan in Laos, Ngo Dinh Diem in South Vietnam—had little support from the people. But our watchword was stability: we paid and trained their armies, and taught their police to put down demonstrations, apparently on the theory that it was more important for these governments to control the population than to serve it.

At times, these governments ran into trouble; sometimes because of their own mistakes, sometimes because of inevitable barriers to political modernization. At times, U.S. support of these governments became a powerful issue around which to organize opposition. But, given our past support, their futures became our responsibility. Their setbacks became our embarrassments. Each increase in turbulence was matched by an increase in our own presence. Aid led to military supplies, which led to military advisers, and then to planes and bombs and troops. The obvious case of this pattern is Vietnam, but it is not the only one. We came perilously close to massive military in-

152

volvement in Laos in 1961 and 1962, before accepting the concept of a coalition government. Had the Korean opposition to Syngman Rhee become a protracted insurgency, instead of succeeding swiftly, we might well have fought there. And today, in Thailand, there are more American troops assisting that nation than there were in Vietnam at the beginning of 1965.

If we expect our military presence to insure stability in Asia, we are deluding ourselves. Many of the nations are passing through the most difficult periods of modernization, in which patterns of centuries are being challenged by political doctrine and new economic patterns. It is pure foolishness to think that disorder, a natural process of change, can be somehow stopped in Asia. It is equally foolish to confuse all such disorder with outside aggression or political subversion.

Our interests, therefore, lie in localizing these disruptions, insuring that they do not become threats to world stability through the intervention, whether by design or accident, of any major world power, including the United States. I am not advocating disengagement from Asia. I believe, however, that it is distinctly in our interest to substantially reduce our military influence and to redirect our political efforts to meet more effectively the forces sweeping Asia today.

SITUATIONS OF STRENGTH

A review of Asia today shows no justification for American military intervention once the war in Vietnam is over. On balance, the Asian nations themselves have been able to cope with indigenous insurgencies. The Malaysian government (with British assistance, it is true) overcame the Communist insurrection which first began in 1947. It has now dwindled to a few hundred guerrillas in the high jungles on the border of Thailand, fighting part time and farming part time. The anti-government activity in Burma is largely confined to parts of the country over which the central government has never been able to assert authority; and the rebellion is divided between competing Communist movements, and tribal rebels who have nothing to do with Communism. The Huk rebellion in the Philippines, once the most substantial threat to any Asian government, was effectively combatted by the late President Ramón Magsaysay, with little outside help; it is resurgent today, but its roots are clearly domestic, not external. The same combination of military counteraction and social reform, which beat the Huks a decade ago, is still available to the Philippine government if it chooses to use them.

Even in Thailand, where reports of guerrilla activity in the North are increasing, prospects for security appear good. Despite attempts to parallel this activity with that of the National Liberation Front of South Vietnam, and despite our movement toward supplying the same forms of military assistance, vital distinctions exist. Thailand is not beset by the national, regional, and religious differences which plague Vietnam. It has a long-rooted monarchy and national allegiance which Vietnam lacks. It has a history as an independent nation, fused with a stable pattern of peasant land ownership. Indeed, the insurgent "Patriotic Front" has gained a foothold only in the Northeast; and the

154

fighting has been done largely by people who are Laotian, not Thai, in derivation. The guerrillas do not have the leadership necessary to expand their insurgency. Nor are the people of that area partial toward the guerrillas. Rather than wishing to overthrow the central government, they seem to want it primarily to provide them more of the economic help they need to better their living conditions.

Nor is the announced intention of Great Britain to liquidate its military presence in Asia a valid reason for us to increase ours. At most, it would necessitate a naval presence or a troop potential in response to emergencies; a task our Seventh Fleet and our airlift capability could perform with ease.

If we look at Asia dispassionately, then, we see nations probably equipped to handle immediate threats (the failure of South Vietnam to meet its insurgency by itself may tell us more about the popularity of that government than the strength of aggression in Asia).

In my view, our policy should reflect this capability. These nations should be treated as self-sufficient equals, not as wards we must preserve from danger. As for the insurgencies which may come, they stem from causes far too deeply rooted for us to erase. The range of weak governments and unsound systems yet to be revealed, the unfulfilled hopes and unresolved conflicts, the pervasive poverty and discontent—these are the facts of life across Asia. And guerrilla movements, despite their use of terror and violence, will frequently offer discontented people a faith, an organization, and a way of life. To these people, the terror which we abhor is not that much worse from the life of poverty and pestilence which they seek to escape.

155

(As Douglas Pike notes in his study of the National Liberation Front, selective terror against unpopular officials may even increase support for guerrilla movements.) It is, to put it bluntly, not our business to suppress these movements, especially if, when we do so, we simply secure these nations for the mandarins and the landlords.

Nor should the United States assume that its national interest is threatened because an insurgent movement adopts the "Communist" or "revolutionary" rubric. On a continent as poor as Asia, the rhetoric of Marxism has considerable appeal. It appears to promise swift modernization, and it is posed as an opponent of "colonialism," which to Asians has been such a painful reality. President Sukarno of Indonesia, long before he allowed the Communists to gain a foothold in his government, preached revolutionary socialism as a method of implementing the national revolution.

But we should remember that Communism in the sense of an extension of Russian and Chinese power, is an offense to Asian revolution, for it conflicts with the most powerful political force in Asia today: nationalism. The same desire for freedom from foreign influence that spawned anti-colonial movements in Asia has also frustrated or blunted Communist efforts. We saw this in the bloody anti-Communist Indonesian revolution in 1965–66, a movement led by nationalists. We saw it in the bitter anti-Chinese riots in Burma, after the overseas Chinese had demonstrated for Mao. We saw it when Chinese military intrusion into India galvanized a pacific nation into military mobilization. Today Cambodia, and even North Korea and Mongolia, defy and denounce Communist China.

156

Nationalism, then, is the best ally against Communist expansion in Asia—far more effective than American armed intervention. But it will be effective on its own terms; not as an adjunct of American power. Nationalism asserts itself against *any* outside power, including ours. If we maintain our massive military presence in Asia, we raise the risk that these independence movements will focus their resentment—and their insurgencies—against *us*. To understand the movements in Asia today, then, is to understand that massive power is no posture for those, like ourselves, who seek peaceful progress.

WHAT ABOUT CHINA?

The strongest argument for maintaining our military strength on its present enormous scale is the fear of China. For some, Communist China today occupies the same position in Asia that the Soviets did in postwar Europe. To them, China is a self-proclaimed revolutionary stronghold, threatening the stability of every non-Communist Asian nation.

I agree that should China embark on a series of expansionist moves throughout Asia, our military assistance would be required. No Asian nation, however free and dynamic, can hope to resist the force of a Chinese army. But is this Chinese expansionism, which has been presented as the root justification for our heavy Asian military force, a present or likely condition in Asia? Is the "China Peril" concept a reality on which to base a foreign policy—as

157

opposed to a last ditch device to scare Americans into backing a policy that has lost its other justifications?

If we look only at China's rhetoric, the danger is apparent. Caught in the grip of a tumultuous "Cultural Revolution" designed to restore pure revolutionary zeal, China now preaches revolution around the world. Defense Minister Lin Piao, in his famous tract in September 1965 branded Asia as one part of the worldwide "countryside" which would move against the established "urban centers" of the world. We could, if we were shortsighted enough, rely on this propaganda as an excuse to remain militarily entwined in Asia.

But if we look at what China has *done,* rather than what she has *said,* the portrait of a force hell-bent for trouble fades. Since the Korean fiasco, the only overt act of Chinese conquest has been Tibet. It was a brutal, tyrannical act; one which demonstrated the repressive character of the Chinese regime. But Tibet, we should remember, has been regarded by all Chinese governments, including Chiang Kai-shek's, as a territorial part of China. Moreover, the Chinese assistance to revolutions has not matched her words of encouragement. In Vietnam, as many have observed, China appears willing "to fight to the last Vietnamese." She has not sent a single soldier. Nor did she come to the assistance of the Overseas Chinese in Burma or Malaysia during recent disturbances. She has not even sought to capture the offshore islands of Quemoy and Matsu.

In sharp contrast to postwar Europe, where the Soviet armies were entrenched in the Eastern European nations they subsequently absorbed, China has no troops deployed outside her borders. Indeed, her biggest fear seems to be for the security of her own borders, which she sees as menaced by American military forces. Where China feels that her own borders are threatened, she may act. Otherwise, the record does not support the vision of a China conquering her way across Asia. This is not to say that China may not turn expansionist. The outcome of her internal convulsions cannot be predicted: she may turn outward. But it appears on the evidence that we need not continue our immense military presence simply because of China's conduct.

China has mighty armies, but their strength is in defense. They cannot move across long distances, nor across the mountains and seas that separate them from most of the Asian lands. The Chinese navy and the Chinese air force, both quite small, could not transport these troops nor supply them during a prolonged war of aggression. China was able to send troops to Korea because supply routes, including a railroad, ran from Manchuria across the Yalu River. But if she has not sent volunteers to Vietnam, despite the importance of the struggle there, despite her desire to outdo the Russians, she would hardly send armies over the mountains to Burma or Thailand or over the sea to Indonesia or Malaysia. Whatever verbal encouragement the Chinese might give to Asian insurgencies, what counts is what she *does*. She has not committed her troops to wars of liberation in other countries.

Nor is China's nuclear capacity yet a threat. Certainly, compared to the might of her two key adversaries, the United States and the Soviet Union, China is in no position to begin a campaign of nuclear blackmail. Given her fear

159

of outside intervention, the last thing China would do is to threaten her neighbors with her nuclear capacity, for China knows that would, as it should, bring an American *nuclear* presence to her borders.

China, moreover, must realize that the world is backing away from the use of nuclear weapons—even the diplomatic use—to settle disputes. Recognizing political realities, China has, despite her spurning of the Test Ban Treaty and the non-proliferation pact, pledged not to engage in a nuclear first strike. This is evidence not of China's passive nature, but of her recognition of the facts of life. We cannot rely on her word, but if she engages in the kind of aggressive diplomacy that could only be backed up by breaking that pledge, she would be inviting action by the other major powers, unilaterally or through the United Nations, to destroy her nuclear capacity.

It is still true, however, that a new Asian policy for the 1970s must come to grips with China, not just militarily but politically and diplomatically. Whether or not she is a military threat, China is clearly the crucial element in our ability both to ease our military presence, and to formulate wise policies toward the other nations.

A major part of the problem is that China is a mystery to us, a vague spectre of hundreds of millions of Communists, fanatical in their hatred of the United States and committed to our destruction. We know far too little of her leadership, her economy, the way her people live and, most unfortunately, of her political intentions in Asia and elsewhere. For this ignorance, China herself bears a major part of the blame. For years she has rebuffed our offers to exchange scholars and journalists—and with the turmoil of the Cultural Revolution, Chinese-American contacts have almost totally ended.

But we must also remember that the United States was for years unwilling to face up to the existence of a Communist regime in China. To suggest the search for a *modus vivendi* was all but treasonable. Our shock at "losing" China (as though it was somehow "ours"), was so great, and created such deep wounds and divisions in this country, that all normal discussions froze up. Men whose judgments we rely on today were pilloried for their small connection with our China policy of the late 1940s. In the 1950s, a United States Senator, *not* Joseph R. McCarthy, grilled a State Department aide unmercifully because he had said the Department had "considered" the question of China's recognition. The hapless aide had to explain again and again that he had only meant the Department had "considered" why recognition was unacceptable.

It is only very recently that public figures have begun to question seriously the vitality of our China policy. Only with a 1963 speech by Assistant Secretary of State Roger Hillsman did a government official publicly speak about the fact that the Communist regime was here to stay. Until then, official American government doctrine was that the Communist regime in China was a "passing phase." Not until the Senate Foreign Relations Committee hearings in 1966 was there any public airing of alternative policies toward China. The decade of silence has left its mark. Although we are acquiring a growing mass of information on China, there are precious few scholars in the United States with knowledge of China and her attitudes.

Given China's hostility toward the United States, it is

natural to want to respond in kind. But we cannot plan Asian policy for the 1970s without consideration of China. She is a crucial power in Asia; she has a quarter of the world's people; she has nuclear weapons and will be able to deliver them within ten years. China's cooperation is vital for our Asian hopes; for if China is not to remain peaceful, neither will Asia, and neither will we.

Clearly, the restructuring of a China policy will require public acceptance. Just as in civil rights, foreign aid, and East-West trade, public officials and spokesmen must now begin the arduous process of discussing China without hysteria, and without easy preconceptions. The emotion surrounding the issue of China has rendered the democratic process of debate largely immobile. Now the time for dialogue has come.

Two years ago I suggested as a first step that the President order a blue-ribbon commission to study the broad question of China and the American attitude toward her. Commissions, of course, do not solve problems. But they do suggest solutions, and point the way to action. This was true of the Civil Rights Commission under President Truman; it was true of the Gaither Committee which studied our defense posture in 1958–59, and it has been true broadly in both foreign and domestic policy.

This commission would be assigned the historic task of examining the basis for more normal relations with China. While immediate prospects are dim, it could create conditions for relations once the hysteria of "cultural revolution" has passed. It could spur the greater study of China by scholars. And it could also free this issue from the straitjacket that has encased it for so many years.

A fresh look at China does not mean any abandonment of our genuinely vital interests, or our commitments to Burma, Thailand, Malaysia, Taiwan and other nations of Asia. It does not mean that we would stand by in Asia if China became expansionist; nor does it mean that we can blind ourselves to the fact that China's present stand toward the United States is one of remitting, almost hysterical, hostility. Of course, it takes two sides to make a lasting peace; but it only takes one to take the first step. And the interest of a peaceful Asia is too important for us not to take this step.

Two immediate areas provide possible means of reviving contact with China in the years to come. First, every effort must be made to bring China into international arms control negotiations. This is so for purely practical reasons: there can be no effective arms control without Chinese participation. If we do not make every effort to come to an arms agreement with China, we will have placed great pressure on India, Japan and other nations to press ahead with nuclear weapons development, or we will find ourselves extending a "nuclear umbrella" of protection around the world, adding new commitments to our burdens. Even with China's disdain for international arms control, we must continue to urge her participation. If China refuses, it will be dramatic evidence that it is China, and not ourselves, which is blocking effective control of the weapons of destruction.

Second, we ought to attempt a relaxation on our total trade embargo with China, and seek the creation of a limited trading relationship in clearly non-strategic goods. This embargo is little more than a symbol of hostility. It

163

deprives China of nothing; for what she does not buy here, she buys from England, France, West Germany and Japan. The fact is, that for all of China's anti-capitalism, more than half her trade is with non-Communist nations. Such a first step might prove the wedge that opens the door to normal relations. Major American companies were doing business in the Soviet Union a decade prior to recognition.

In addition, we should seek to increase contacts—both official and unofficial—with China. At present, our only link with China is through informal ambassadorial discussion in Warsaw. These contacts have been rigid, formal affairs with little exchange and no results. And even this meagre contact has diminished. We should try to begin a diversity of discussions with Chinese diplomats in Paris, Geneva, and other capitals in the hope that they may result in something more. Further contact—particularly among private citizens —is one possibility. If we offered to allow medical personnel, such as heart specialists like Michael DeBakey and immunologists like Jonas Salk, into China, her refusals would become more difficult to maintain. From this start could come a regular exchange of scientists, professors, artists, athletes and even tourists. What limited security risks may exist—and they are doubtful in view of the initial hostility and attendant watchfulness of security agencies in both countries—are far outweighed by the chance to begin some contact between our two societies.

Finally, we should begin to move toward some resolution of the United Nations membership question. Today, China—with more people than any other nation—is the key nation outside of the UN. This absence renders much discussion of Asian problems irrelevant. For no Asian question is complete unless China's role is understood by all.

No one can argue that the United Nations has been more effective with China out. We have kept her out partly from spite and partly in the hope that ostracism would make her behave in a more civilized way. It has not done so.

Each year the United States expends precious diplomatic capital to secure votes in the UN to block China's admission. Each year—at least until the internal explosions turned some nations away from accepting China—more and more votes were won for China. In 1965, the question of Chinese admission resulted in a tie vote (although two-thirds were needed). Further, because of our position, the question of admission has always been placed in the form of expelling the Formosan government and substituting that of mainland China. Many of our traditional allies—Great Britain, India, the Scandinavian countries—have supported this move. Such a vote, if diplomatic conditions change, could imperil what I believe is an important task of insuring the continued representation in the UN of the 12,000,000 citizens of Formosa.

Perhaps China does not want UN membership. Perhaps it would be in our interest to keep this shadow play in motion. But I do not think it wise to risk Formosa's expulsion and prevent the voice of a major world power from being heard. Instead, I would suggest we propose to admit both Chinas into the United Nations.[1] To prevent the Security Council seat from clouding the issue, I would

[1] There is precedent for this, where single nations have split and the United Nations handled the problem by allowing membership to both: in 1947, when Pakistan separated from India, and in 1961 when Syria withdrew from the United Arab Republic.

165

propose further that neither China have this seat—China's permanent place could be turned into a revolving seat reflecting international conditions which have developed since 1945, or the number of permanent Council members would be reduced from five to four. The UN machinery can, as did the League of Nations, provide for future expansion of the Council so that China—if she did not act to frustrate the work of the UN—could ultimately gain the Council seat. In addition, the use of the veto could be sharply reduced on the Council, to further reduce the risk of renewed Chinese intransigence.

I am aware that both Chinas have rejected similar proposals. I believe, however, that Communist China will begin to understand the need to participate in the international community. Perhaps this goal is a long way off. But an Asian policy for the 1970s cannot ignore China; neither can it regard China as a shadowy threat. We have seen in the past how relations among nations can change. The portrait of a Stalinist Russia committed to our destruction has faded; we now understand that we can live at peace with the Soviet Union. This realization was a journey of many steps—from the 1955 Geneva conference to Khrushchev's visits to Europe and the United States to a test-ban pact. And it had many setbacks—the U-2 incident, the fiasco of the Paris Summit, the Cuban missile crisis.

Nor can China stand still. The forces of change are at work there, as in every country. The veterans of the Long March to the caves of Yenan are now old, their revolutionary experience is not that of the 700,000,000 other Chinese whose devotion to the cause must be stimulated artificially. Utopian promises have faded, a Great Leap has stumbled, and a self-imposed isolation is having its toll on industrial and scientific progress. There is surely going to be a leadership change, as Mao Tse-tung fades from the scene. Policies such as I have recommended could accelerate this evolution of China toward a posture that would benefit world peace. Whether or not the impasse with China is resolved, the United States must learn important lessons to develop a new Asian policy. Above all, we must learn the lesson of restraint. We should hold down our commitments, not because we do not care what happens in Asia, or because, impatient, we seek to disengage ourselves, but because our power there is limited and can often do more harm than good.

THE NEED FOR RESTRAINT

I have already suggested that our military involvement should be scaled down; but we should also recognize that Asian nations fear economic as well as military power. It is tempting to proclaim the dawn of a new era in Asia, and attempt to usher in that age with lavish economic assistance. But the fact is that such assistance is useless, even harmful, without a clear understanding of what such aid will accomplish. Nowhere, for example, were we more generous with our aid than in Laos in the 1950s. This tiny kingdom, carved out of the Geneva Conference on Indochina, received more than $235,000,000 from us—including more per capita military assistance than any other nation in the world. Guided by ludicrously inaccurate intelligence—we believed for months a false government report that Laos had been invaded—U.S. assistance helped breed rampant inflation, and spawned a climate of anti-Americanism that helped pro-Communist forces triumph in national elections. In its 1959 report, the House Government Operations Committee observed:

"The aid program has not prevented the spread of Communism in Laos. In fact, the Communist victory on the slogans of 'government corruption' and 'government indifference' might lead one to conclude that the U.S. aid program had contributed to an atmosphere in which the ordinary people of Laos question the value of friendship of the United States."

This is the danger of overextending aid. Its use—and misuse—links us to whatever regime is in power, and limits our ability to identify with legitimate revolutionary movements. Aid programs must be divorced from political support of established regimes. American aid must assist, not hamper, the efforts of national governments to chart their own course.

We must have a much greater understanding of conditions in Asia. Many of our worst mistakes, as in Laos and in Vietnam, have been the result of poor intelligence. We reacted to dangers that did not exist, because we knew too little about the culture, the ethnic groups, the historic factions and tensions in Asian countries, and how they would react to events and policies. Our personnel in these countries must end their dependence for intelligence on the elite groups who do not see or are not sympathetic to the people below their social class. The great masses of people in Asia are gaining in political power. They can no longer be ignored.

Further, we cannot work with Asian nations in building independence if our own hands are not clean of colonial practices. Our professions of self-determination may, for example, be undercut by our continued domination of Okinawa and the Ryuku Islands as a military protectorate. Whatever military functions the Islands have, we do not need political control to retain military bases. We retain the military use of many bases in several Asian nations through voluntary agreements. If these Islands are returned to Japan, our ability to work with other Asian movements will be greatly enhanced—and our own real interests in Asia promoted.[2]

Similarly, our political stance must not be dictated by the American private investments injured by Asian nationalism. To halt the long-term assistance for a nation because of expropriation is only harmful—for it deprives us of the opportunity to negotiate settlements, and damages the prospect for further investment. Most Asian governments today recognize the need for foreign investment. They are trying to work out ways to make it acceptable to their people. We should not object if they choose to impose reasonable controls and profit sharing arrangements, and remove some of the special protections our business now has. It is no more than we would do if we were they. It is in our own self-interest. For if such adjustments were resisted, private American enterprise could easily become

[2] Our refusal to make this concession during Premier Sato's visit to Washington in the fall of 1967, coupled with our gratuitous offer to surrender control of the Bonin Islands—with a population of only two hundred—was a backward step, and will cause severe embarrassment for a Japanese government that has been one of our staunchest Asian friends.

169

the symbolic issue which could sweep a truly radical government in, and our business people out.

The same principles should guide our foreign aid in Asia. Increasing amounts should be channelled through the Asian Development Bank and the Mekong River Coordinating Committee, which are under UN sponsorship but controlled by the Asians. This would end the resentment that comes with bilateral aid. It could also extricate us from a serious foreign aid dilemma we face in Vietnam when hostilities cease. That country—North and South—will need vast sums for reconstruction. But other Asian countries need it as well. Those which stood with us in Vietnam will want priority over equally needy nations which did not. In 1947, we told the European nations to decide for themselves how to divide the money of the Marshall Plan. It would be easier for us, politically, to let these hard decisions on who gets what be made by Asian development institutions.

A ROLE FOR JAPAN

Crucial to the aid problem, as well as our other hopes in Asia, could be the role of Japan. In twenty-two years, Japan has recovered from the war to become the third industrial power in the world. She is by far the strongest, richest, most stable and dynamic nation in Asia today. She is the best illustration to Asians that prosperity can be achieved without losing freedom, and she could do much to advance the peace of the area.

Japan has a natural reluctance to assert political leadership in Asia. Her last foray into international politics was disastrous. But she is beginning to move out of her shell. She is sending her own young volunteers to do Peace Corps work in Asian countries. Her decision to fund the Asian bank indicates she is beginning to realize that, for her own sake, she must help in the critical problem of Asian development. Japan conducts $6,500,000,000 in trade with other Asian nations each year. She is the closest industrial country to what is potentially the richest market in the world. It is in her interest to involve herself fully in Asian stability and development.

Japan can play a leading role in Asian solutions. She can be a bridge, as well, between Communist and non-Communist nations. She, along with countries like South Korea, Taiwan, and the Philippines, which have overcome the most difficult of development problems, can take over the role of providing educational and technical assistance that the nations of Europe had to vacate. They can do it more easily than we, because they do not carry the white man's burden.

In summary, our Asian policy after Vietnam should stress political and economic rather than military efforts, Asian solutions rather than American solutions. The posture I am suggesting is not one of isolation. It is, rather, one of realism. It is a stance which will recognize what we all know—that we cannot, and we should not, impose our world view on distinct, diverse, and alien cultures. We can hope, for example, that Asia will move toward regional cooperation—a movement indicated by the 1966 formation of the Association of Southeast Asia, and by the renewed interest in linking Indonesia, Malaysia, and the

171

Philippines. We can hope for the growth of Asian peace-keeping forces, and regional efforts in health, education and agriculture, led by the developed nations such as Japan and Malaysia. We can cooperate with such efforts, offering our resources and our skills.

But we cannot call a Westernized Asia into being; we cannot think that Asia would be better if the thousands of years of cultural and social heritage were erased, to be supplemented by a Western outlook. We are not missionaries; we do not carry the Gospel. Our own difficulties, and our past mistakes, should warn us of the danger of smugness.

The medieval monk, Thomas à Kempis, once said, "Be not angry that you cannot make others as you wish them to be, since you cannot make yourself as you wish to be." Asia is a place where we can work, as friends and as equals, to provide better lives for the Asians. It is not a place to watch easy illusions crumble into hard—and bloody—reality.

LATIN AMERICA—AN
APPROACH

In some parts of the world, talk of "the next critical few years" is simply rhetoric. Faced with social and economic patterns of centuries, it is neither wise nor practical to base a foreign policy on assumptions of rapid and sweeping change. Grandiose commitments of progress, large infusions of capital, may well do more harm than good.

In Latin America, however, we face a continent where decisions *are* imminent; where the coming decade *will* be critical. Here, as on no other continent, the 1970s will determine whether we are right in asserting that fundamental and rapid change can take place without violent, bloody disruption. We have pledged to the continent of Latin America that change with order is possible; and some of the best political men of this hemisphere have made that same pledge to their people. All we do over the next decade must be aimed at fulfilling that pledge.

It is fashionable to speak about the "underdeveloped countries," or the "poor countries"; and although such descriptions describe common poverty which afflicts most of the Southern Hemisphere, they also mask the fact that each continent, and the countries within each continent, differ enormously in culture, customs, problems and prospects. No part of the developing world holds as much promise and danger for the future of Western civilization as does Latin America. From the American Indian cultures of the high altiplano, to the Europeanized civilization of Santiago or Buenos Aires, there are important differences among the American republics. Certain generalizations, however, can be of great relevance to American policy.

Alone among the developing continents, Latin America is essentially Western in its culture and values, and Catholic in religion. Its philosophical and ideological roots, like our own, spring from Europe. Its countries have been independent for a century and a half. This is both an asset and a handicap. On the one hand it promises a strong sense of national identity resistant to external subversion and helpful to development, while on the other it afflicts many countries with deeply embedded social institutions—oligarchies and military establishments—which are often a barrier to progress. Latin America is not only a part of our hemisphere and therefore of great strategic importance to the United States, but also for most of its history we have been, and remain, the dominant power in the Latin consciousness. In this, too, it is unique in the world.

Many of the countries of Latin America, and some of

174

the most important, are on the threshold of modern, developing economies. Two of the three largest, Mexico and Argentina, could, with luck and effort, leave the ranks of underdevelopment within a decade; while the largest of all, Brazil, with 40 percent of the area and population of the continent, larger than the continental United States, is underpopulated and rich in unexploited resources.

Certainly there is danger that unrest in Latin America may bring hostile governments to power. It has happened before. And hostile governments in our own hemisphere would have a profound and dislocating impact on the United States. But if the dangers are great so are the possibilities. For with development and growing strength and self-confidence, Latin America, alone among the developing continents, may some day take its place as an equal contributor to Western civilization, along with North America and Europe. More than a billion people, inhabiting the most fruitful part of the globe, sharing a common culture and common values, joined in safeguarding and pursuing a peaceful world community, is indeed a vision and hope worthy of the best efforts of the best among us; and of the full energies of the United States of America.

Moreover, our concern with the reconstruction of postwar Europe and defense against Soviet power and ambitions has turned American attention away from Latin America. While the Marshall Plan was pouring billions into Europe, we virtually ignored the deepening poverty and revolutionary ferment of our fellow American Republics.

The jeering and dangerous mobs which greeted Vice-President Nixon on his trip to Latin America awoke the United States to the grim realities of Latin American discontent and growing hostility. Then the triumph of Fidel Castro in Cuba brought home with a shock the reality that the danger we had been combatting across the width of two oceans was a reality on our own doorstep. We began asking why; and what we should do.

We looked south—and saw a continent plagued by widespread illiteracy, poverty, non-existent education, and, in some countries, feudal, backward economies that kept millions of people in serfdom. We saw nations in which almost half the adult population could not read; nations, like Peru, where 2.2 percent of the people owned 70 percent of the land; a continent that was spending only 2.8 percent of its output on education, and where infant mortality rates, outside of large cities, exceeded 70 percent.

What these figures show in cold print, I saw in human terms during my visit to Latin America in 1961. In Recife, Brazil, I saw men and women sorting through garbage in search of food. In Cali, Colombia, I saw a school where only 200 of 780 children could meet the entrance requirement: a pair of shoes. I saw men with no roof to shelter their families, women and children living in the streets by stealth and wit—and a boy who had been sold by his mother, who could not feed him. And I saw a medical report of industrial workers, living in a modern housing project. Ninety-five percent had intestinal parasites; 40 percent had hookworm; 60 percent had roundworm; at least 40 percent were "dangerously ill."

Similar conditions exist in most Latin American countries. To change these conditions will require far more patience than we have shown in the past. We will have to remember that in Latin America terms like "capitalist" and "socialist" have many and varied meanings, and that a Latin American "rebel" may be a follower of Mao, or simply a believer in the economic measures of the New Deal. In short, our Latin American policies in the 1970s—in view of our past and of our "special pledge" to the continent—will test our maturity, our compassion, and our vision as the greatest power in the Western Hemisphere.

THE COMMUNIST THREAT

An important first step is to put the "Communist menace" into proper perspective. A legislator can win headlines by pointing to active, radical left-wing movements in most Central and South American nations. In this way, all movements of social change may be labeled "pro-Communist," and our policy can develop along the lines of repression and intervention. But an examination of "left-wing" movements in Latin America will reveal that most of them have no interest in advancing the aims of Soviet or Chinese policy, and that those that do are not doing very well.

The Cuban missile crisis taught the Russians the dangers of posing a threat to U.S. security in the Western Hemisphere, and it now appears safe to say that this direct form of Soviet intervention is not likely to recur. While there are both legal and underground Communist parties with pro-Soviet attitudes in Latin American countries, the fact is that the leadership of these parties is, for the most part, tired, old, and bureaucratic. In Cuba, for example, the Communist party at first attacked Castro's guerrilla war as "adventuristic." Not until Castro succeeded did the old-line Communists join him. Moreover, the Soviets have been far less interested in sponsoring Latin American revolutions than may be assumed. The Russians have diplomatic relations with Venezuela and Colombia, which fought Castro-type insurgencies; they have even extended credits to right-wing governments. The split between Russians and Latin Americans is apparent—so much so that the revolutionary Latin-American Solidarity Organization barred the Soviet Union from participation in its activities.

Nor does China pose any immediate threat to the peace of Latin America. Its rhetoric is, of course, solidly behind the immediate and violent revolution of Latin American nations against the United States and its "puppet" governments. But China is half a world away, preoccupied with internal turbulence, and lacking the resources to support revolutions. It is clear that the vehement language of Chinese support will attract university radicals, and it is likely that we will see the growth of pro-Chinese wings of Communist movements in Latin America. Indeed, there are already Soviet-Chinese rifts in countries where the Communist party is legal. China probably gives some token support to these schismatic movements. Yet it is unlikely that the Chinese can either control or dominate Latin American radicalism.

What is the extent of Cuba's involvement in the "export" or revolution to its Latin American neighbors? It is clear that she backed and financed some guerrilla activity, notably in Venezuela, as the Organization of American States concluded in its 1967 investigations. However, most of these guerrilla movements are on the run; their ranks severely

178

thinned; their prospect of success dim. They have, in most cases, been defeated or eroded by the vigorous activities of popular democratic governments, such as that of Venezuela, with little help from us except for training and equipment. The fate of the Bolivian guerrilla movement, and the death of Ernesto "Che" Guevara, shows that it is difficult, and perhaps impossible, to "export" revolution; that even with help from the outside, only indigenous forces, relying on real grievances and local leadership, can hope to summon the necessary support among the people. Moreover, there is a deep tradition of non-intervention in Latin American politics, which Cuba has offended. In fact, ever since the Cuban missile crisis, Castroism as a revolutionary force has been on the wane. If new revolutions come they will, I believe, be sponsored by indigenous leaders.

I do not mean to be complacent about the prospects for violent revolution. Radical revolutionary movements, subject to Communist influence, might succeed in a Latin American country, and vigilance is necessary. However, if we assume that all radical movements are subversive; if we curtail aid to governments because they promise swift change; if we deprive them of our markets and our resources, we ourselves may force them to look elsewhere. The spread of indigenous Communist states, however independent, would clearly mark a grave setback in hemispheric cooperation. We can live with a hostile government in Cuba. It would be far more difficult if the Cuban example was duplicated, for example, by Argentina, or Colombia, Peru or Brazil. Violent revolution—and the growth of violent insurgency in the hills of Bolivia, Guatemala, Ecuador, and Venezuela—would threaten or eradicate democratic progress, and with it the aspirations of Latin Americans who revere independence and freedom.

THE REAL LATIN CHALLENGE

The challenge, then, is not simply Communism; it is to turn the Latin American revolution toward democratic, rather than totalitarian forms. The means for achieving this goal are set forth in the Alliance for Progress. For all its slow development and unrealized goals, the Alliance remains the most promising and realistic policy for hemispheric cooperation. The responsibility for failures in its implementation must be borne by the United States and Latin American governments alike. Yet the principle of the Alliance for Progress—that we must play a supporting role in the Latin American revolution—remains valid. If, in the past, we have played too great a role in shaping policy, in the future we must keep firmly in mind the needs of the nations we are pledged to help. In a hemisphere of twenty nations, ranging from the fifth largest in the world to small slivers of land, no wholesale prescription can realistically meet the problems of all of them. The history of the continent is diverse; and the United States cannot hope to succeed in its aims if it regards the entire continent as an amorphous mass.

Our assistance, therefore, must be linked to significant reforms within the nations themselves. At the founding of the Alliance, with the Charter of Punta del Este in 1961, the participating nations pledged themselves to radical change, including "more equitable distribution of national income"; "comprehensive agrarian reform with . . . a more equitable system of land tenure"; tax and currency reforms and increased efforts in health, housing, and education.

Some of the record is encouraging. In Chile, President Eduardo Frei is working against great obstacles to introduce radical tax and land reform programs. In Peru, President Belvande's *Cooperacion Popular* has given people in more than three thousand communities the chance to improve their own lives by building cooperatives, market roads, and improved public health facilities. Similar reforms are underway in Venezuela and Colombia.

Yet reform has been slow. *Latifundistas* still reap the profits from the land tilled by *campesinos*. The wretched slums which dot the large cities of Latin America—the *favelas* (or *villas miserias*) grow, and some in the ruling group are indifferent to the plight of those who live in such misery. The hard work of tax reform has often been neglected. Many of the wealthiest pay lower taxes than do our citizens who earn $10,000 a year, and until 1966, no one in Latin America had ever been jailed for tax evasion. Moreover the improvement of rural areas—where millions dwell wholly outside their national life—has been severely neglected.

Of course the United States cannot tell other nations how to run their governments. But we can design our aid program so that our resources go to the nations making needed effort. Teodoro Moscoso, the first administrator of the Alliance, and a man with deep commitments to Latin American autonomy, observed:

"You can hardly expect U.S. taxpayers, already heavily burdened, to help underwrite development programs in countries where a few privileged people, far richer than the average U.S. taxpayer, are virtually free from taxation. Nor is it reasonable for North Americans, brought up in the tradition of the Homestead Act, which offered 160 acres to every family able and willing to work them, to perpetuate agrarian systems where a handful of wealthy families own as much as 90 percent of the desirable land . . ."

We cannot betray the principles of the Alliance—"to unite in a common effort to bring our people accelerated economic progress and broadened social justice, within the framework of personal dignity and individual liberty"—by turning our aid program into support for unjust economic systems. Currency stabilization, trade help, business investment are all improvements but they will not succeed unless they are linked to popular participation and fundamental social reform. A Latin American Common Market will help business; but it will not, except over the very long run, help the peasant who is totally outside the money economy, nor those who work for slave wages across the continent.

The U.S. has spent $9,000,000,000 and the Latin nations ten times that much since the Alliance began. In the future, our limited resources should be directed toward efforts designed to change the distorted social structures of these countries. For example, in Latin America college education is usually free; high school education is not (and in some places it is non-existent). Clearly this benefits the relatively small group with funds to support early education. We should, then, stress technical assistance programs and capital funds for the building of free secondary schools

182

—along the lines of programs now underway in Peru and Chile. We should assist agricultural diversification and productivity; the fact is that per capita productivity is lower today than it was ten years ago. Another 85,000,000 acres of land must be brought under cultivation, just to maintain the now-inadequate production. Such assistance —with direct tools and skills in rural areas—would be of benefit in bringing new hope to those now fighting a losing battle for mere survival.

In short, our assistance should be aimed not only at increasing economic growth *per se,* but also in bringing the benefits of growth to those who most need it. Our help should, as I have said, be consonant with the premises of the Alliance for Progress in that assistance without substantial internal change is neither helpful nor warranted. In this, our greatest allies will be men like Eduardo Frei of Chile, Fernando Belvande of Peru and Raul Leoni of Venezuela who have been laboring to bring about peaceful reform within their own countries.

THE DEMOCRATIC LEFT

We must also take stronger sides in the critical battles for political power between the democratic and the oligarchical and military forces. In a few countries a powerful oligarchy dominates much of the economy, while in others an alliance of the wealthy and the military dominates the political life of the nation. In the past, we have often associated ourselves with the oligarchy and the generals. They offered stability; they professed anti-Communist and

183

pro-capitalist sentiments; and they welcomed private investment at terms favorable to American industry. But these forces are also in large measure responsible for the rampant injustice which discolors the life of Latin America. And in a time of rapid change they will almost inevitably be swept aside. Our policy must therefore be to develop a fruitful association with forces which will supplant them and remain our friends.

Luis Muñoz Marín, former governor of Puerto Rico and the architect of its remarkable growth, has said that "the one group in Latin America which understands the depths of revolutionary ferment . . . and which can provide responsible leadership to shape this revolution into constructive channels is the democratic left. The well-meaning democratic conservatives, men whom we can often respect, have no real grasp of the revolutionary surge, and are, therefore, powerless to compete with the totalitarians."

There are two crucial reasons why the democratic left must have our special sympathy. First, it offers an alternative to violent revolution which can—possibly—accomplish the task of making a peaceful revolution. Second, it constitutes the one group in Latin America which represents our own best impulses toward the continent: the hope that social justice and individual liberty can become a permanent reality in Latin America.

What I have said does not mean that we should intervene in elections to help our "friends." In addition to corrupting democratic processes, such interference would insure the defeat of the democratic left. When FRAP—the socialist-Communist alliance in Chile—won 39 percent of the vote in the 1964 elections, its principal charge against

184

the Christian Democrat, Eduardo Frei, was that he was a tool of the Americans. Clearly, the democratic left must not be interfered with in the shaping of its own policies and programs. Yet, if we are willing to cooperate with change, our own interests can also flourish. For example, in Chile, President Frei is trying to "chileanize" the U.S.-controlled copper industry by a gradual increase of Chilean control and he is doing this with the agreement of the American companies. In Peru and Venezuela, governments are seeking to gain increased influence over major utilities that are now in the hands of foreign investors.

It is vital that we understand that this inevitable, natural tendency toward national autonomy is neither a threat to American security nor even to our private interests. We cannot condemn these nations, or cut off our support, just because they trade with the Russians (as do our European allies) or criticize our global policies, or implement their own economic systems. For one thing, Latin support for U.S. international policies is largely a matter of comfort rather than effective aid in achieving our goals.

I would far rather see a dynamic nation, true to the Alliance, which is at times critical of the United States than a stagnant nation which makes no progress but sings our praises. And I believe that, in assessing which nations are the ripest for takeover, totalitarian forces would choose the latter. As a Latin American president once said to an American official: "If you demand a government which says 'Yes, yes, yes'; you may finally get one that says 'No, no, no.'"

ARMIES AND ARMAMENTS

We should, of course, do all we can to discourage military takeovers. Not only do they flout the democratic principles of the Alliance for Progress, but they tear the fabric of constitutional government, making it impossible to establish the atmosphere of stability and orderly change essential to economic development. It is difficult for governments to embark on sensible long-term projects and policies when they live under the constant shadow of a military coup, or must tailor their acts to satisfy a demanding military. If a military regime comes to power, our policy should be governed both by the nature of its acts and the swiftness and sincerity of its effort to restore constitutional government. Where a military government shows a real willingness to move toward constitutionalism, as in Peru in the early 1960s, or itself embarks on a program of serious reform and development, then assistance may be appropriate. There is no automatic answer to such problems. It is a question of degree and of the available alternatives. There is, however, little justification for assistance to a despotic and backward military government; and, however enlightened the economic policies of a government, our words and policies should make clear our disapproval of repressive measures and the deprivation of basic freedoms. In the long run our interests will best be served by making it clear that the United States is acting as a force for freedom in the hemisphere and reserves its warmest support and friendship for those who share democratic principles.

186

Similarly, we must use our influence to slow down the Latin arms race, which is draining away funds desperately needed for social change. Some nations spend more of their annual budgets for arms than for capital investments—more for war than for health and education. Much of this money is for the sophisticated, expensive machinery of modern warfare—jets, warships, and tanks.

This is a tragic waste of financial resources. In a continent which has had fewer wars than any other in modern history, no nation is in danger of attack by its neighbors. And domestic subversion, however real the threat, is not a problem to be countered with sophisticated weapons of wide destruction. It is a danger which can best be handled by trained police and security forces, knowledgeable in using force with discretion and discrimination.

Unfortunately, national pride and prestige—and the strong influence of the military, even in democratic nations—have led Latin nations into this destructive competition. The United States, which formerly contributed to the arms race through aggressive arms sales and a futile policy of "controlled escalation" has tried to discourage such buildups; but Latin American nations have subsequently turned to Europe.

It may be tempting to argue that, since these nations will buy their arms elsewhere, we might as well do the selling. But this ignores both the lessons of the past and our hope for the future. As the principal military force in the hemisphere, we must demonstrate convincingly that our interest in Latin America is no longer one of bases and arms—that our future assistance will be in the direction of social improvement.

187

To that end, I believe the most effective way we can influence the Latin nations to scale down the arms race is to eliminate—altogether—our own program of sales and grants, with the exception of assistance for counter-insurgency. We cannot prevent Latin nations from buying arms abroad, but we can make sure that we are not the suppliers of arms. In addition, we should take the lead in encouraging nations of the Southern Hemisphere to pledge themselves to end the purchase of sophisticated military equipment. Such an agreement—enforced by the Organization of American States—would put Latin America in the forefront of regional disarmament programs.

Arms races on whatever scale are dangerous. To support such a race, even with the justification of neutrality, is dangerous. I hope the United States has learned from its Southeast Asian experience that there are grave dangers in supplying weapons to help governments combat insurgency at home. We may ultimately find two Latin nations battling each other with American weapons, as we did in India and Pakistan. In addition, we might face this consequence, described by a senior military officer in Bolivia:

> "We are certainly not going to supply the means for Bolivian army hotheads to start bombing and napalming villages or even suspected guerrilla jungle hideaways. Civilians would inevitably be killed and we have a long experience that this inevitably produces a stream of recruits for the guerrillas."

AMERICAN BUSINESS

The maintenance and extension of U.S. business investment during the next decade in Latin America will require both ingenuity and serious attention to the fields in
which operations are conducted, the manner in which they
are conducted, and the way Latin workers are treated. In
general, there is less resentment of U.S. ownership of industries in the field of consumer goods than in the field of
public utilities. This is understandable. Americans who get
annoyed at local transit or electric companies would be
more resentful if they were owned, say, by Germans. The
question of ownership of the important mining and extractive industries is a closer one. In general, U.S. businesses which own the only such industry in a country are
headed for difficulty, because of its great significance in
the minds of that country's people.

An effort to construct a working relationship between
the forces of revolutionary change and U.S. business investment in Latin America should be imbued with our support of social reform in Latin America. If we are to avoid
crude and hasty action against U.S. industry, such cooperation is necessary. And even more important, the flow of
private capital is vital to the success of the Alliance and
social progress itself.

The original goals of the Alliance called for
$600,000,000 a year in private and foreign investment. As
we have noted, this rate has not been achieved in the last
two or three years. This means that participating nations

189

are not receiving as much capital as they need for development.

I mentioned earlier that many democratic governments in Latin America may take steps to curb the strength of American investment participating in areas such as public utilities and extractive industries. Half the productive equipment on the continent is owned by American investors; one-third of all Latin exports stem from this source. If strong and industrially sophisticated nations like France and Canada see dangers in U.S. economic power, the suspicion and resentment of the Latins, when linked to our record of political intervention, is understandable. Some Latin leaders have even charged that the Latin American Common Market is a scheme to speed U.S. takeovers, through our superior technology and merchandising techniques.

This resentment and suspicion exists despite the fact the U.S. business firms are, as a group, the most progressive and socially conscious on the Latin continent. Many of them have made impressive efforts in aid of national economies and have assisted in community development. Oddly enough, some radical Latins who want to expel U.S. business are supported by conservative Latin businessmen who believe U.S. competition drives up their own wage costs.

In cases where it seems prudent to change American ownership, there are ways that it can be managed without dislocation. Partial nationalization, mutually agreed upon in advance, as in the case of the copper industry in Chile, is one alternative to expropriation. Another alternative would be for American businesses to become involved in management contracts, which can be profitable but which do not involve ownership.

190

Much will also depend on how American-owned businesses treat their Latin American employees. One constructive approach in preventing discontent would be to provide greater opportunities for stock options, not just to workers but to suppliers as well. Businesses would permit, with government sanction, their shares to be traded on the local stock market. They could sell more of their goods under new Latin brand names instead of U.S. brand names. In short, each way they can identify more closely with the nation in which they operate would help to guarantee their presence and increase their prosperity.

Among the important steps American business can take is to bring into its operations as many Latin managers and technicians as possible. Business firms are the ideal institutions to undertake the vital task of training Latins to run the machinery of modern industry. Modernization of a nation does not just mean building factories and roads and irrigation projects. It means developing the capabilities of the people. When the technical and managerial tasks of development are placed in local hands, the people feel new confidence in themselves and new faith that change is possible. They feel their efforts can affect their own destiny and that of their country.

And encouragement of Latin talent is sound business practice. Every time a *campesino* becomes a consumer, another customer is created for business products. Every local worker who can perform up to the standards of American industry increases the efficiency of the business operation. It is also survival insurance in a revolutionary period. The greater the stake the Latin people have in these operations, the less they will believe that private enterprise means for-

191

eign domination, and the less they will heed the siren song of expropriation.

All these decisions must, under our system, be taken by business itself. But many enlightened businessmen have already demonstrated an awareness that even when short-term losses are involved in some of these policies, if they can win for their companies a respected place in the new society that emerges from the Latin revolution, they will have served the long run interest of their stockholders as well as the nation.

FROM IGNORANCE TO APPRECIATION

Because they require more patience and understanding, all of these suggestions will require a change in the public attitude here in the United States, to which most new foreign policy moves must be acceptable. This will not be possible unless we gain greater knowledge of Latin America, its customs, its cultures, and its importance to us. This greater knowledge implies respect.

For many decades, the chief characteristics of our attitude toward the people of Latin America were ignorance and disdain. We did not take them seriously. There was very little interest in their history, problems or culture, even in the one place it could have been expected, the universities. Even today, six years after the Alliance for Progress, there are few academic centers of real quality for the study of Latin American affairs. College students today perhaps can name one or two Latin painters and composers, but few can name a single Latin poet, or writer, or even a President.

This ignorance has been our loss more than the Latins. The Latin people, as difficult as their life may be today, are members of one of the deepest and richest civilizations on this earth. The art, the sculpture, the metalworking, the way of life of the pre-Columbian era is immensely impressive, as is the culture many other Latins brought from Europe.

But Latin America also has an equally exciting contemporary culture. A Chilean poet won the Nobel Prize for literature. An Argentine painter won the top award at the 1966 Venice Biennale. As seen in Brazilia, São Paulo and Caracas, Latin architecture and city planning are considered to lead the world. Knowledge of Latin culture is important not just as the folkways of another underdeveloped area. It should be an important part of the common knowledge of the educated American. When we isolate ourselves intellectually from Latin America, we not only make it harder to sympathize with its political and economic problems. We cut ourselves off from much of the cultural ferment of the New World.

United States intellectuals have usually been alienated from public affairs. This has not been the case in Latin America. Many Latin intellectuals have been the spokesmen of the peoples' aspirations. Simón Bolivar, Domingo Sarmiento of Argentina, Francisco Miranda of Venezuela were men of letters as well as statesmen, just as was Thomas Jefferson. The young poets and writers and philosophers today, in their coffee houses and universities, have a strong love for their country. They express the hope and longings

G

193

of their people, as well as their bitterness and cynicism. They could help generate the excitement the Alliance for Progress must have for the Latin people.

But I have found that often their understanding of our country is as sparse as our knowledge and understanding of them. American literature courses at many Latin universities end with Edgar Allan Poe. Many of the students and teachers I have talked with still believe old and tired clichés about the United States: Wall Street, lynchings and such. They are unaware of the currents of creativity, freedom and dissent running through our universities and the minds of our young people. They are unaware of the very real achievements of the Alliance. They lack excitement about its potential. It will be difficult, but essential, to persuade them differently.

I think we have learned in the United States, in such fields as race relations and tolerance between religious groups, that sympathy and understanding are the result of personal contact. They come from people rubbing shoulders, learning about each other, melting stereotypes in the heat of contact and discussion. We need to spread, in the United States, an image of Latin Americans that is one of dignity. New efforts are needed to tie the Americas closer together in the realms of culture and education. Our universities, our government and our leaders must join to give our people a greater awareness of the rich culture and infinite possibilities that lie to the South, to show the Latin America of today as it really is.

We should establish, under public or private auspices, a Latin American Cultural Foundation, made up of distinguished men of arts and letters in the United States. Its

194

purpose would be to honor outstanding cultural achievements of Latin Americans. It would offer prizes for outstanding work to writers and artists in a variety of fields, and arrange for exhibition in the United States, or, in the case of literature, translation into English. The recognition of such a Foundation would be of tremendous help to Latin artists in their own countries—and an invaluable aid to our understanding of them.

We also need more teachers, at our universities and theirs. We could do this by establishing joint chairs—for the study of United States civilization in Latin universities and of Latin civilization at our own. I do not mean an exchange program of professors. The holder of the chair of North American studies at the University of Buenos Aires would be an Argentine. The holder of the chair of Latin American studies at the American university would be one of our citizens.

Our involvement and concern with Latin America should not be one which rises in times of crisis and subsides in times of calm. It must be a steady and purposeful commitment. For while revolution, with its conflicts and dislocations and possibilities of bloodshed, is surely ahead, beyond that is the vision of free and democratic nations making a real contribution to their nation and the world.

I would like to see a progressive Latin America, with the United States, uniting in common purpose with our cultural brothers of the nations of Europe, in a real Atlantic alliance of trade and growth and mutual help—a partnership producing for the billion people who would be involved the highest standards of wealth and life; a partnership which would be the strongest force for peace and

195

stability in the world. This may be a vision, but it should be remembered that it was practical visionaries, like Bolivar, Juárez and San Martín, who freed the Latin nations, and who are in the forefront of Latin progress today. The people of Latin America deserve this kind of future. Life will be better for all who border the great ocean of the West if this vision can be attained.

OF WAR AND WANT

For the United States, the most urgent need over the next decade is to help the world remain at peace. For two-thirds of the world, however, the most urgent task is more basic—it is to win the battle for human survival, and begin leading lives of decency and purpose. What we in the United States must understand is that we will not be working fully to secure peace, unless we aid others to win their fight against poverty.

In one sense, our assistance does not depend on our own desire for peace. President Kennedy spoke out of the best American tradition when he said:

> "To those people in the huts and villages across the globe struggling to break the bonds of mass misery, we pledge our best efforts to help them help themselves, for whatever period is required—not because

the Communists may be doing it, not because we
seek their votes, but because it is right."

But it is also true that we can play a powerful part in
preserving peace by helping the world's majority to achieve
better lives than they have now.

If we look at the poor nations of the world today, we
see continuing turmoil. Over the last eight years, there have
been more than 175 outbreaks of serious violence around
the world, aimed at overthrowing existing governments. Almost all of them have taken place in lands where the per
capita income is less than $300 per year. Of the thirty-eight
poorest nations in the world (those with per capita annual
incomes under $100), thirty-two of them have suffered
serious outbursts of sustained violent upheaval.

The violence we glimpse around the world is the product of diverse causes: there is revolutionary nationalism in
Asia—religious and cultural divisions in the Middle East—
tribal wars in Africa—ideological cleavage in India and Pakistan. But all these differences are intensified by poverty.
When nations are poor and people miserable, there will
be insurgencies and disorder; and governments will mount
aggression against neighbor nations to divert their peoples'
attention from the hopelessness of their own lives.

Poverty by itself does not breed war. Indeed, if we were
callous enough to seek a world where stability was the only
virtue, we would seek to keep nations in abject poverty. It is
only when people begin to glimpse the prospect of a better
world—when they understand that the dreary, joyless lives
of their fathers and brothers is *not* the only way of life—that
they begin to demand a share of human decency. But even if

198

we wanted to betray our claim to humanity, we could not do so. The "revolution of rising expectations" is irreversible. Around the globe, long-dormant people now understand that they are not doomed to misery. They will seek change; rapid, sweeping, total change. And they will get it, whether in the form of peaceful evolution, militant revolution, or destructive violence.

Our role in this process should not be that of a benevolent despot. Aid without prudence and understanding will help neither the people of the developing world nor ourselves. But properly designed, our efforts and assistance can accelerate development and help preserve the peace; for we can provide funds to begin and complete projects, and the skill to prevent the promise of development from becoming frustrated. To fulfill this role, however, we shall have to change both the level and the nature of our assistance.

The coming decade will be a harsh one for the two-thirds of our planet which lives in poverty. Production of food in Asia and Africa has not kept pace with the population. The prospect of widespread famine in these continents seems a reality. These nations are desperately seeking food imports; but at the same time they may not be able to pay for those imports, since the goods which form the bulk of their export earnings are bringing lower prices on the world market, or are facing competition from other nations. And even as the spectre of collapse becomes grimly real, the gap in living standards between the rich and poor grows larger. Last year, the national income of the United States grew by $40,000,000,000. This increase was more than the *total* national incomes of India and all of black Africa combined—700,000,000 people.

India is a dramatic illustration of the crisis we face. For years we have been told she is the crucial testing ground of whether a poor nation can develop under conditions of freedom. After three five-year plans, after immense efforts by her planners and her people, the results in human terms are dismaying. Since 1946, India's real economic growth—the difference between her increase in wealth and increase in population—has been one percent a year; an average increase in income of 70¢ per year per person. India has 12,000,000 unemployed workers; fully 60,000,000 were affected by last year's famine. With economic discontent a major factor, the last election produced a stunning repudiation of the Congress Party, which has governed India since her independence. A majority of India's states are now in the hands of opposition parties, and political stability is threatened. A good harvest this year has softened the atmosphere of crisis, but underscored India's excessive vulnerability to the forces of nature.

India, and the other nations of poverty, are remote from us. But so was Vietnam a decade ago. If the discontent triggered by poverty sparks widespread anti-American revolutionary movements in Africa and Latin America, and if hostile governments exploit discontentment in other lands we may find ourselves either impotently witnessing a disastrous shift in the balance of power, or else embroiled in ceaseless war. If we ignore the link between government failure and violent insurrection, we do so literally at our peril.

What of our efforts to aid development? We have done

much and have won successes. The recovery of Europe, however special a case it was, is an achievement in which we can justly take pride. So is the self-sufficiency of Turkey, Taiwan and South Korea. But looking to the world today, we have not done enough. Despite rising populations and growing needs, the total amount of public development capital moving from all developed nations to the underdeveloped world has remained static at a little more than $6,000,000,000. And in the United States, support has slackened. Since 1962, foreign aid budgets proposed by Presidents Kennedy and Johnson have been slashed in Congress by 20 to 30 percent a year. In 1967 the program was cut to little more than $2,000,000,000— the smallest amount since the inception of foreign aid in 1947.

The process of development in the world is not going well. Despite our foreign assistance—more than $100,000,000,000 since the start of the Marshall Plan twenty years ago; despite regional and international programs; and despite the heroic efforts of the poorer nations, there has been no measurable improvement in the lives of most of these people. In some countries, plagued by rapid birth rates and inadequate growth, the standard of living has actually declined.

Foreign aid must be increased; it must be expanded; but it must be understood. The current rationale for foreign aid—as a tool to fight Communism—is crumbling. The roots of this rationale for aid go back to the late 1940s. Facing strong opposition to the novel concept of foreign assistance, President Truman recognized that aid would have to be "sold" in clear political terms. And it was Michigan

201

Senator Arthur H. Vandenberg—the man who led the Republican Party out of isolationism—who advised Truman that to win his fight for foreign aid, he would "have to scare hell out of the country." We have done that now for eighteen years. Our Secretaries of State, our Presidents, have repeated over and again that foreign aid was a method of stopping the spread of Communism. The need for healthy economies, independent nations, and moral imperatives were all acknowledged; but in general foreign assistance was supported by the argument that we could buy off potential Communist expansion with money, and if we did, we could avoid the need to fight it off with troops. This rationale, in turn, locked our aid program into the confines of the cold war.

The results of this identification were harmful to the foreign aid program in many ways. First, it diverted much foreign assistance into military purposes at the expense of economic development. Since 1948, more than half of our foreign aid has been in the form of weapons and other military assistance. Money that could have gone to irrigate a valley or build a health center has gone to prop up a general or strengthen a corrupt and unpopular regime. Thus, the United States, the first nation in history to offer its treasure to others for help and hope, became the biggest arms supplier in the world.

Further, our economic assistance was channeled not to the places where development needs and opportunities were greatest, but where the Communist threat was considered strongest. Last year, the AID budget proposed more money for South Vietnam than for all of Latin America. In Africa, where small investments can yield great returns, our assistance virtually ceased—in part because the "Communist threat" no longer seemed severe. Kenya, with our help, could achieve major breakthroughs in farm technology and cooperatives. But our assistance has all but disappeared; for the Communist menace is not strong enough in Kenya to justify aid under our present rationale.

We have, in addition, loaded our programs with political restrictions which undermine some of our most important development efforts. There is, for example, no more hopeful project in Asia today than the international development of the Mekong River Basin. It holds the promise of energy for industry, irrigation, flood control, and agricultural improvement—energy which will help 30,000,000 people. Despite their mutual hostilities, the four nations of Southeast Asia—Thailand, Laos, Cambodia, and Vietnam—are working on it jointly. Yet last year our government had to withdraw its support for a Cambodian dam which was a key to the entire Mekong project, because Cambodia had sent food to Hanoi, and we categorically bar aid to nations which trade with Hanoi. Similar restrictions on aid to nations which trade with Cuba, or in other ways assist the Communist world, are equally foolhardy, for they block the very development our aid is designed to assist.

Moreover, these poor nations can only regard such a restrictive aid program as a club, employed to bludgeon them into supporting our foreign policies. This perception is so prevalent that nations like Burma and Cambodia, desperately in need of help, have all but ended American aid because they feel it jeopardizes their national independence. Nations may be poor; but they are nonetheless proud; they do not wish to be wards of a wealthier country. They do not want aid if it is tied to a UN vote or support for another nation's foreign adventures. They are the architects of their own national interest; they have no desire, any more than would the United States, to bind themselves to the political prerequisites of foreign capital.

Thus has the anti-Communist rationale for foreign aid harmed the program. Whatever the practical need to sell foreign aid with this explanation, such a basis will no longer work. For one thing, as recipient nations turn leftward, or if assistance fails to stop Communist penetration, it will be aid which is blamed—since it did not do its self-proclaimed job of stopping Communism. Further, if the *détente* with Russia grows and if China continues to shun an expansionist role, there will be no basis left on which to support foreign aid. The receding Communist threat may well take with it our program of assistance itself—long before it has accomplished its real purpose, and at a time when it is desperately required.

A NEW RATIONALE FOR AID

We must, then, understand our own interest in providing foreign aid. In addition to strengthening the security of nations, its key role is to contribute to the peace of the world, by accelerating development along peaceful paths in the poor half of the world.

Let me be clear. We dare not repeat the mistakes of an earlier rationale by establishing sweeping assertions. Aid cannot "buy" peace any more than it could "buy" friends for America. There will be violent insurrections; there will be insurgencies, and they will take place even where the United States provides aid. But we clearly can—and clearly should—use our efforts to keep the promises of modernization, thus tempering bitterness and frustration among the people of poverty, and hastening the day when poverty and misery no longer feel the fires of discord.

A NEW AID PROGRAM

Such an assistance program must be based on a clear strategy of development, linked to the needs and tasks of developing nations. Aid cannot be turned on and off to equal the "threat" to a nation or its cooperativeness with the United States. It must be a long-term program, with long-term appropriations, so that poor nations may know the level of assistance they may expect as they plan their own development efforts.

The first requirement of such a program is increased funds. Per capita aid to India, for example, has come to only $3 per year. We—and the other developed nations—have not made the effort we pledged; our promise in the United Nations to devote one percent of our national production to foreign assistance has not really been met; for our accounts include Social Security payments to former American residents living abroad, as well as high-interest loans which are useless for nations without capital. Even the $6,000,000,000 level of aid from affluent to poor nations is misleading—for the poor nations have had to pay almost half of this amount back in interest and amortization on past loans. Moreover, as import needs of poor nations have risen, they have been drained of more foreign exchange than they received in aid.

The consequence of inadequate aid is apparent in Africa. That continent has been forced to absorb far more than its share of Congressional cuts in the aid budget. Under an elaborate rationale of development emphasis, we eliminated our aid programs in twenty of the thirty African nations. To further mask our parsimony, we tried to encourage regional development projects. In addition to causing political dilemmas (it would force nations like Guinea, which has declared its independence from France, to return to the French orbit to participate in aid benefits) such a move only destroys the credibility of giving effective regional projects.

Given the need of developing nations to project aid they receive into long-range planning, I believe we ought to recognize that these nations can use—now—at least $4,000,-000,000 a year more than they receive. To make this possible, I would hope that the developed nations should agree—now—to achieve a transfer of one percent of their gross national product to world development programs by 1970. For the U.S., this would mean a doubling of the present level of aid. We can readily afford this. Surely the effort to build a peaceful, more just world is worth what we spend each year on toys and cosmetics.

In addition to increasing our effort, we should direct much of our aid through multilateral channels. Bilateral aid is in many respects stifling. It identifies the donor with too many of the political aspects of the recipient. It is surrounded by the aura of charity—and it can frequently breed resentment, especially where a wealthy, white Western power is the source of funds. Bilateral aid is still needed where social reforms can be thus encouraged in no other way. But a greater multilateral effort would enable our funds to be properly used without entangling us in political difficulty.

Organizations such as the World Bank and the International Development Association have had wide experience in administering programs; they have stringent checks to prevent corruption and abuse of aid funds. With increased resources, these organizations could adequately staff and supervise far more projects. If we channel our assistance in the next decade increasingly through such organizations as the World Bank, the UN Development program, and regional development banks, we can begin to coordinate the methods of foreign assistance with its real purpose. As a further demonstration of this interest, we might urge the Soviet Union and other Communist nations to pool their resources with us, in aiding a nation like India.

To make these programs work, we must adjust our other economic policies to make them consistent with the aims of our aid program. Astonishingly, much of the aid we give today is in effect erased by other policies we pursue. In order to understand this, we must realize what foreign aid does in purely economic terms: it increases the amount of foreign exchange a poor nation has to buy the things it needs. Assistance is one way of getting such exchange; another is by exporting goods and attracting foreign money (say, through tourism). But most wealthy nations pursue a welter of policies which drastically cut down on the for-

207

eign exchange of poor nations—in effect, canceling out the assistance.

THE ROLE OF TRADE

For example, trade policies of rich nations prevent developing nations from increasing their trade. The Common Market, with its high levies on agricultural imports, and our own tariff bars and import quotas, are powerful frustrations to countries whose trade we seek to build up through aid. We know, as the European nations told us fifteen years ago, that trade, not aid, was the key to economic health. The poor nations today are in that same position. Since 85 percent of their export earnings come from the sale of primary (i.e., mineral and agricultural) products, increased trade is a crucial element in economic health. Yet our policies fail to recognize this.

Latin America provides a striking example of this indifference. Since 1954, we have made some $12,000,-000,000 in aid available. But, despite pleas from top Latin economists, we have failed to promote vigorous trade in key goods. Consequently, the money Latin America received from exports of coffee, copper, rubber and other commodities declined by $12,000,000,000. In terms of money available for development, then, we in effect wiped out our own aid.

No matter how many factories or electrical grids we build, we will not help nations develop self-sufficiency if they cannot sell their wares to nations that use them. We cannot promote modernization, then, unless we open trade possibilities for all the nations of the world—not just the wealthy.

Similarly, the rise in the cost of exporting has eaten into the poor nations' foreign exchange. They have, through massive effort, increased exports by 6 percent a year. But the net gain in export transactions has been halved between 1960 and 1966—from $2,700,000,000 to $1,100,-000,000—by the rise in shipping, insurance and marketing costs, by higher repayments to foreign firms, as well as by service costs on past loans.

Finally, we have not worked hard enough in the field of price stabilization. Of the eighty underdeveloped nations of the world, almost fifty of them depend for foreign earnings on the export of one or two crops or commodities. Far more development money comes from such exports than comes from foreign aid. But in recent years, the steady drop in world commodity prices has crippled development efforts. Colombia, for example, which used to be able to count on about $500,000,000 in foreign exchange from coffee sales each year, had only half of that last year—and its development, as a consequence, has been cut by a third. The ambitious social reforms of Chile's Eduardo Frei were set back substantially because the world market price of copper declined by 25 percent in one year.

A realistic goal linked with assistance would be to increase export earnings of poor nations by 6 percent each year. To meet this goal, the trading nations of the world should erect price stabilization agreements on commodities such as rubber, tin, cocoa, tea, and petroleum. These agreements—similar to the Coffee Agreement of 1963—will provide foreign exchange with a minimum of political dislocations—for the funds will come from trade. Until these agreements are completed, the International Monetary Fund should expand its grants program to nations dependent on one or two commodities—thus providing a cushion against a drop in the world market price of what they sell. In addition, the Common Market would, hopefully, cooperate in the lowering of agricultural products from developing lands; and wealthy nations would protect poorer ones in any international schemes to increase world liquidity, the working capital of world trade.

Within the United States, a coordinated series of policies will require a reappraisal of the network of restrictions we have erected for the benefit of our own industries. Tariffs and quotas are part of this reappraisal—but so are the laws which require recipient nations to buy the goods in the United States and ship them in American vessels—restrictions which lower the value of aid by almost 20 percent. So are the webs of subsidies we give to domestic business, that make it harder for poor nations to compete in our market. Congress must adjust the tariff laws to give preferential treatment to the agricultural exports of poor countries. It should also consider President Johnson's suggestion at last year's Latin Summit Conference that their manufactures receive some preference.

Changing these policies might involve temporary dislocations in some parts of our economy. But the last few years have shown how expansionist, and remarkably flexible, the American economy has become. Millions of jobs have been destroyed, through automation, geographic shifts and changing defense needs—but even more jobs have been created. Domestic industries that might be adversely affected by the policy changes I have recommended should be eligible for the same adjustment assistance as the Trade Expansion Act provides—but I think these industries would be very, very few.

PRIVATE INVESTMENT

In any large scale program of assistance, public funds and public policies are not enough. We must, consequently, encourage private enterprise to join in the development process. Even if the wealthy nations double their assistance levels, that will not meet the needs of the poor nations for development funds without vast amounts of additional capital from private investment. Those nations which have enjoyed successful economic growth—Korea, Mexico, Venezuela, Taiwan, Malaysia—are countries which have encouraged local and international private investment.

The kind of investment needed most is in agriculture. For unless the developing world can greatly increase its food production, through the kind of technological revolution we have had, the people of this world are, very simply, going to starve. The grim pattern now taking shape in India, in which all foreign capital must be diverted from capital development to food to avert starvation, must alert us to the critical need for rapid agricultural modernization.

It is private investment—by the giant "agri-businesses" of the developed world—that can change this. They have learned how to increase production, develop better crops, conserve soil, and fully use available water. They can help establish buying and selling cooperatives, and pricing sys-

211

tems to permit farmers in poor nations to use their resources in developing new techniques.

Government can assist these firms, by providing guarantees against risk, similar to the loan given to the New York City bank that is supervising the modernization of agriculture in Thailand; interest subsidies for long-term loans between private firms and government, and cutting bureaucratic delays in investment procedures.

THE NEED FOR PATIENCE

Finally, an assistance program geared to rapid, peaceful development will require patience. Impatience is a natural response when effort does not produce immediate results. We have engaged in foreign aid for twenty years. But we should remember that fifty years after American independence, nine out of twenty-five states were in default in their own obligations. The French have a saying that "it takes three generations to make a Frenchman." That is not an unreasonable time to create a world that is economically healthy. Of all the nations in the world, only Japan was able to modernize in a shorter time.

More important, the achievement over the last 20 years has been great. A decade ago, South Korea was crippled by war, impoverished and despairing. Today, it has one of the highest growth rates in Asia—8 percent since 1963. It has increased its farming potential, laid the groundwork for industrialization, and held its first free, peaceful general election. In Taiwan, growth rates of 8 percent have also been achieved, and agricultural growth has doubled.

212

In Pakistan, food output has doubled after a new farm strategy was implemented. India, despite its troubles, is achieving success in greatly increasing grain yields. Other continents show similar breakthroughs. Fifteen years ago, Kenya was emerging from the terror of the Mau Mau rebellion. Today Kikuyu farmers, settled on freehold farms purchased for them from European owners by the British government and the World Bank, are producing record crops. The more adventurous are branching into dairying. In West Africa, the Volta Dam, finished a year ahead of schedule and at $15,000,000 below the contract price, is producing the cheapest power in the world and industries are coming in to use it.

These few examples show that patience need not be blind. Growth and development over the next decades will take place, provided we keep faith with the aid programs, which have made these rapid advances possible.

I hope it is clear that I do not believe foreign aid, by itself, will preserve the peace of the world, or improve the lives of its citizens. Political disputes, corruption and indifference in governments, war by inadvertence—all of these disasters are no strangers to this world. No aid program can guarantee prevention of human folly. In addition, aid in itself will not change unjust social structures, nor protect the peace. The process of modernization must be a fundamental one of social as well as economic change.

Nations will not aid other lands when the effect is to entrench a class system and make the rich richer. Farmers will not be inspired by shiny new machines if they do not own the land they till. Commodity agreements will not help if the higher prices go to growers who salt the money away

213

in foreign banks. Educational aids will not bring learning to those deprived by caste or class from going to school. Peaceful change is still change; it requires, on the part of all nations, a willingness to extend opportunity to those who have never known it. We cannot force this pattern on rulers; but we can design an aid system, as we began to do with the Alliance for Progress, linking our aid to self-help.

To help preserve world peace through world development is an immense task. But in principle and philosophy, it is no different from what we have done in our own country. Since the beginning of the century, we have known that the greatest source of domestic discord and danger lay among those who lived in poverty. But where they have been given a chance to rise, their increasing demand for goods has been the surest foundation of a healthy economy. Fifty years of government effort, from Wilson's New Freedom to the New Frontier and the Great Society, have resulted in a redistribution of wealth to the underprivileged. This, in turn, has increased everybody's wealth and created the strongest economy the world has ever known. So there is nothing revolutionary or untried in this approach.

And I do believe that the battle for humanity can be won peacefully. To fight that battle is to honor the best of our heritage. John Adams said at the outset of this republic that America was a providential act, designed for the benefit of the poor of this earth. Our young people have made it clear that they accept that heritage—their work in the Peace Corps has been one of the most inspiring examples of practical idealism this world has seen.

Now—as we approach the 1970s—nothing could more capture this spirit than if the young generation took for themselves the task of assisting this modernization process. Having at their command the wonders of affluence and the skill to employ those wonders, this generation could well redeem its manifest idealism if it acted—as individuals helping other human beings—to bring those skills beyond our borders, to develop industry, to irrigate the fields, to teach children to read and write.

There is more to this challenge than the preservation of world peace, vital as that is. There is the creative explosion of whole cultures. The people of these nations are poor, but many of them belong to some of the oldest, most creative traditions on this earth. If those now bound down by poverty could use their talents and historic cultural abilities to the fullest, they could make this world infinitely richer and more exciting for all of us.

The poverty which now scars half the world is also at our doorstep. It will not let us be, however we wish it. As Pope Paul said in his encyclical on the development of peoples, "If today's flourishing civilizations remain selfishly wrapped up in themselves, they could easily place their highest values in jeopardy, sacrificing their will to be great to the desire to possess more."

The younger generation understands this danger. They want the challenge of tasks left undone—and no task is more challenging, more fulfilling, and more necessary for a peaceful world than the task of helping half the world's people lead better lives. It is a task worthy of a decade—and of a generation.

APPENDIX: A PROPOSAL FOR REFORM
OF THE DRAFT

In the chapter entitled "The Need to Serve" I argued that
the present system of selective service must be replaced by
a more modern and more equitable system. The present draft
method fails to provide a rational, efficient program for selecting the minority of eligible young men who actually enter
military service. Further, today's draft has discriminated on
social, economic, and occasionally racial and political grounds;
and it introduces injuring uncertainty into the lives of young
men and their families.

The Senate Armed Services Committee has recognized the
pressures created by the growth in our population, and the
inequality inherent in our present system. Under the provisions of the bill,[1] reported by the Senate Armed Services Committee to the Senate in June 1967, the Selective Service System
will be permitted to institute a system of random selection as
soon as it has developed a workable one. The bill reported
by the House of Representatives, however, prohibited Selec-

[1] S.1432, 90th Cong. 1st sess. (1967).

tive Service System from moving towards any random Selective Service System without first submitting the plan to Congress for approval. This requirement, seemingly reasonable on its face, is tantamount to an outright prohibition, given the unalterable opposition to random selection of House Committee Chairman, Mendel Rivers, and a ranking Democrat, Edward Hebert. Both of these legislators have announced their unalterable opposition to random selection.

Unfortunately, it was the House version which prevailed in the Senate-House Conference Committee attempting to reconcile this and other differences between the two bills. The House provisions prevailed in virtually all the differences.[2]

In my testimony to the Senate Armed Forces Committee on April 13, 1967, I presented the bare bones of a workable system of random selection of draftees and expansion of that presentation follows:

PERSONNEL REQUIREMENTS AND AVAILABILITY

In the next few years, about 1,900,000 young men will turn 19 each year. Of this number about 600,000 will either be declared ineligible for military service, on mental, physical or moral grounds, or will receive hardship for other legal de-

[2] This was due in part to an unusual parliamentary situation in the Senate, where the debate over the censure of Senator Thomas Dodd was taking place. The Senate-House conferees were under pressure to bring a bill to their respective chambers before the law expired on June 30, 1967; yet the Senate leadership was reluctant to permit the Senators to be absent from the Floor of the Senate for any length of time. In fact, the debate on June 14, 1967, on acceptance of the conference report was limited to two hours, by unanimous consent—hardly a suitable length of time to probe all the difficult issues raised by the conference report. This debate was the only one permitted to interrupt the proceedings on the motion to censure Senator Dodd.

217

ferments or exemptions. This leaves about 1,300,000 young men eligible and qualified for induction each year.

Estimates made by the Defense Department indicate that about 570,000 young men will voluntarily enter enlisted service each year. This is 110,000 short of the total estimated annual enlisted needs of 680,000 men, and 730,000 less than the total number of eligible young men. It means that 110,000 must be drafted out of 730,000 available.[3] The figures look like this in tabular form:

Number turning 19		1,900,000
Disqualified		600,000
Eligible		1,300,000
Enlisted Requirements		680,000
Volunteers		570,000
Non-Volunteers	730,000	
Draftees needed		110,000
Monthly need		9,200

In sum, after Vietnam and without the demands of another similar conflict, we will have a yearly need for 680,000 enlisted men each year, 570,000 of whom will be volunteers. The remaining 110,000 must be draftees, and they must be selected from the 730,000 non-volunteering nineteen-year-olds.

HOW RANDOM SELECTION WOULD WORK

Under this particular random selection proposal, the director of Selective Service will continue to receive monthly manpower "calls" from the Secretary of Defense, just as he

[3] This 110,000 annual figure for draftees is about 9200 per month, considerably below the 34,000 call for January of 1968. It must be noted that the 34,000 represents the demands of Vietnam; the lower figure, the demand of a normal peace-time situation.

218

does today. The Defense Department will determine the size of these calls from our troop needs, from enlistment rates, and other figures.

Then the director would assign each state a quota of draftees which that state must produce. The quota would be a figure derived from pro rating the total U.S. need among the states on the basis of the eligibles in a state. Once again, this procedure is similar to existing practice. Each state would decide for itself how best to produce the quota from among the local draft boards within each state.

Although I have used the existing state quota system to explain this role of the director, I believe it would be fairer to use national or regional quotas to determine draft needs. Given the disparity in the treatment of young men with similar backgrounds by different states—such as Peace Corps volunteers—a random selection system might well incorporate a broader geographical basis, preferably national, to replace the state quota system.

But perhaps the most important of the director's functions, under this random selection system, would be his random structuring of the days of each month and the letters of the alphabet. He could do this by computer, by lot, or by any other of a wide variety of methods.

This is the heart of the random selection system. The days of each month would be scrambled, and the resulting sequence would determine the order of induction. For example, the scrambling for January might put the 21st first, the 10th second, and perhaps the 9th last. Those young men born on the 21st of January would be almost certain of going; those born on the 9th almost certain of not going. Those born on the days listed in between would have a very good idea of whether they would be called, as the number needed from any given geographical area would be publicly known, as would the number of available men and their birthdates.

Some jurisdictions have large numbers of residents and a breakdown by days of the month may not be sufficient. The director of Selective Service would then scramble the letters of the alphabet, arranging them in a random sequence. This would be used to choose among those born on the same date, if such a choice need be made.

The director would arrange the days of each month and the letters of the alphabet at least six months in advance of the actual month, in order to minimize the hardships in the planning of careers and lives of our young men. This could be done very simply by twice yearly scrambles, one March 15 and the other on September 15. In the March scramble, the sequences for the next following September-March would be determined. In September the March-September sequences and so forth.

Under this proposal, the director would have the new responsibility of arranging an induction sequence by lot, the fairest of all possible means, and then announce the sequence. He would continue to receive monthly draft calls from the Defense Department, and would promulgate rules, regulations and policy, all of which are within his present duties.

ROLE OF THE LOCAL BOARDS

The local boards, which now number more than 4000, would continue their present role of registering each young man on his eighteenth birthday and for examining him during his eighteenth year for physical, mental, and moral qualifications.

The local boards would, in addition, be responsible for granting the deferments which would continue to exist under the proposed new system: hardship, medical, ministerial, high school. However, no student deferments would be permitted beyond the twelfth grade. Further, occupational deferments would be virtually abolished since almost no nineteen-year-old has developed the critical skills necessary to justify an occupational deferment.

220

Having examined all its registrants, and declared some fit for military service and some not, the local board would then be left with a residuum of eligibles greater by a factor of seven than those it needed to meet its quota. It would choose which of the eligibles should be drafted by using the sequences determined by the director of Selective Service, and would apply them to the group of registrants who turned nineteen in a given month.

If, for example, the March quota for a local board were seven men and it had forty-nine eligibles (men who qualified and who would turn nineteen in March) it would notify the first seven of their incipient inductions. The remaining forty-two would then be placed *below* the men turning nineteen in the following month, April. Thus, the forty-two not selected in March would never be selected unless all the April eligibles were selected without satisfying the quota—a very unlikely event. Under this system the youngest eligible men, early in their nineteenth year, would know what induction obligations they were under and would not be subjected to long periods of uncertainty or fruitless waiting.

The problems of those whose deferments expire after they have turned nineteen—as with high school students—are not difficult. When a young man loses a temporary deferment he is not thrown into the pool of eligibles for the month he loses it. Thus, his exposure to the draft lasts for one month and on the same basis as other eligibles.[4]

This proposal has one defect which also plagues our present system: bunching. January is a heavy enlistment month, because many young men who could enlist in October, November or December wait instead until Christmas. For similar reasons, July and September are heavy enlistment months, July being

---

[4] Some critics have pointed out that a man born on the 31st could lose his deferment in a month or thirty days, but in that instance he either could be deemed to be born on the 30th, or be required to draw a number between 1 and 30 for the purposes of the draft.

right after school graduation and September after the summer. In any month of heavy enlistment, draft calls are low. The reverse is also true. Thus a twenty-year-old high school student graduating in late June would, under this proposal of a random selection system, be put in the July pool of eligibles, even though his birthday was in March. His chances of being drafted might be less in July than March, thus introducing an element of discrimination, for using high school graduates over dropouts. To avoid this problem, all nineteen-year-olds might be put into the pool during the month of their nineteenth birthday and if one of those selected were deferred, then he would be inducted at the termination of his deferment. Once the system was operational, this problem of drafting extra men to fill the slots of those with deferments would disappear, since deferments would be terminated in every month, and it would, in all likelihood, average out.

CONCLUSION

Such a system would work. It would increase predictability and reduce uncertainty. It would increase fairness and reduce the incidence of arbitrary decisions. It would increase efficiency because of its simplicity. Finally, it has great flexibility to meet changing manpower needs.

I do not claim that the random selection system I have just described is either flawless or the best which could be devised. Nor do I suggest that an all volunteer army would be presumably undesirable. But as long as the need for a selective service system continues, a random selection method would be fairer and more efficient than our present system.